# Think
## and Make It
# Happen

## DR. AUGUSTO CURY

THOMAS NELSON
*Since 1798*

NASHVILLE   DALLAS   MEXICO CITY   RIO DE JANEIRO   BEIJING

Published in Nashville, Tennessee, by Thomas Nelson. Thomas Nelson is a registered trademark of Thomas Nelson, Inc.

Thomas Nelson, Inc. titles may be purchased in bulk for educational, business, fund-raising, or sales promotional use. For information, please e-mail SpecialMarkets@ThomasNelson.com.

Unless otherwise noted, Scripture quotations used in this book are from:
HOLY BIBLE, NEW INTERNATIONAL VERSION®. © 1973, 1978, 1984, by International Bible Society. Used by permission of Zondervan. All rights reserved.

Scripture quotations marked KJV are from the King James Version.

To protect the identities of the people whose stories are told in this book, some names have been changed and some circumstances altered. However, all of the contextual elements and results are absolutely true.

### Library of Congress Cataloging-in-Publication Data

Cury, Augusto.
  Think and make it happen / Augusto Cury.
    p. cm.
  Includes bibliographical references.
  ISBN 978-0-7852-2781-6 (hardcover)
  1. Thought and thinking. 2. Thought and thinking—Religious aspects—Christianity.
3. Success—Psychological aspects. 4. Success—Religious aspects—Christianity. 5. Intention.
6. Quality of life. I. Title.
  BF441.C87 2008
  158.1—dc22                                                              2008039609

*Printed in the United States of America*

08 09 10 11 12 QW 6 5 4 3 2 1

I, _____,

dedicate this book to _____.

Navigate the waters of your inner self with emotion.
Turn the simple things into a spectacle for the eyes.
Never give up on life or on those you love.
Never grow old in the territory of emotion!
Disappointment, frustration, and loss will always occur,
But work through each pain as an opportunity to grow.
Find an oasis in each of your deserts!
Contemplate beauty. Unleash creativity.
Manage your thoughts. Protect your emotions.
Live an enterprising lifestyle.
Train your amazing mind to be brilliant. You deserve it!


Date _____

# Contents

# Introduction

One of the great ironies of being human is that we pay the most attention to the things that, in the long run, matter least—and vice versa. We expend great energy taking care of our homes, cars, clothes, property, and money, and far less energy taking care of our most precious possession: our lives, and especially our mental health! Yet without an excellent quality of life, all the rest is meaningless.

My research and observations of people over two decades and in many settings have led me to a sad conclusion: we humans are collectively becoming more mentally and emotionally ill. By "ill," I don't mean physically sick or mentally insane, but living far beneath our great potential to attain real quality of life. That quality of life can be achieved by using the tools that we already have within us, and especially by learning to *think correctly*, which will be the focus of this entire book.

Why do I use the term "think correctly"? What do I mean by titling this book *Think and Make It Happen*? Our mind controls all. It is who we are, the height of all our being. It has enormous potential and power—far beyond what we imagine or typically access in our day-to-day lives. And it has the ability to radically influence all that we say, do, think, and feel. So when I was looking for words that describe all we can be, that would properly capture the idea of reaching our full height mentally and emotionally and socially, the words that kept surfacing were: *think correctly*.

And though I call it "think" correctly, my term entails our emotions and personalities as well, not just our thoughts, for as you'll see in the chapters ahead, the mind is really our control tower—the source of every word we speak, every action we take, every emotion we feel, and every thought we have. By abiding by the twelve principles I explore within this book, you'll be training yourself to think in a way you never thought possible, and thereby achieve the extraordinary quality of life you desire and deserve. By harnessing the power of your mind, you can do, have, achieve, and create anything you want for your life. You can truly *make it happen.*

Let me give you an example by offering a contrast. An "ordinary" thinker—my term for someone who simply lives day to day but does not seek to make the most of himself—drives his car and takes care of his bank account, but a person who thinks correctly goes beyond that, not only taking care of the physical and material necessities but also managing his thoughts, leaving the audience and becoming the director of his life script, and authoring his own story, which I'll explain within this book. An ordinary thinker reacts before considering the possibilities, but someone who thinks correctly engages her mind first and then responds rather than reacting. She empathically puts herself in the place of others and exercises emotional intelligence, almost "seeing" feelings even when they are not obvious. An ordinary thinker protects his house by buying insurance and installing a security system, but a person who thinks correctly protects his emotions as well, and he also exercises his creativity and makes a habit of contemplating beauty. These and many more ideals are qualities of a mind that thinks correctly.

Don't let the terminology throw you, however. Though we might believe that thinking "correctly" is exclusive to a few gifted individuals—attainable only by the elite—that is simply not true. Every person can learn to think in this way. And we need to, because thinking this way is our greatest tool in the fight for our psychological well-being and happiness.

A mind that thinks correctly follows clear goals and exercises self-control without being controlled by the environment, circumstances, or inner conflicts. A correctly thinking mind uses its worst days as a story line, if you will, to write the most important chapters of its life project. That's what happened to me. In the midst of a depression in my early years of medical school, I realized one of the keys to developing a creative, secure, and stable mind and healthy, peaceful emotions—all of which lead to the quality of life that we long for. That key involved understanding that *when the world abandons us, the loneliness can be overcome, but when we abandon ourselves, the loneliness is almost unbearable.* Said another way, when we consciously give up on ourselves, or simply remain passive and never invest in developing our potential in the first place, our mental health and happiness will be destroyed in a hurry. At that time of great psychic struggle, I recognized I had a choice, and I chose the path that has made all the difference—the path to real quality of life.

Likewise, for those of you who long for something far better than what you're experiencing now, this book contains a strategy that will not only encourage you on your journey but equip you with the principles you'll need to manage your life, thoughts, and emotions at a high level. And my story, as well as those of numerous people I've worked with, will reinforce those ideas.

The psychic earthquake I went through in medical school encouraged me to get to know the fantastic world of the human mind—that complex universe inside each of us—beginning with my own. I began to think differently, reflect, analyze, and inquire. I literally asked thousands of questions regarding how the mind works. Some of them I've been unable to answer even after decades of investigation and research. But I believe that I've found a few important answers. From them I've extracted the fundamental Think Correctly principles that are the subject of this book. And they address our greatest societal and personal ills.

## Six Paradoxes—and a Solution

As I've already said, people usually develop ordinary minds, although they have the ability to develop extraordinary minds. Because we do not exercise and develop the potential of our minds, we are experiencing six great paradoxes within the human race—paradoxes that my work has shown result from the failure to fully achieve the mind's potential:

1. *Sadness and anguish are increasing.* Never have there been so many resources available that were intended to bring us pleasure and joy: television, music, sports, video games, the Internet. Yet in spite of being constantly surrounded by entertainment, we are sad and discontented.

2. *Loneliness is spreading.* With exploding populations like those of China and India, which each now have as many people as were in the whole world at the end of the nineteenth century, you'd think no one could be lonely. Yet we live as a world of intimate strangers, having managed to isolate ourselves from our neighbors and coworkers with the conveniences of modern life. Though technology has given us access to people anywhere in the world, most of us are lonelier than we've ever been.

3. *Dialogue is dying.* It is common for us to communicate through electronic media about impersonal topics. When it comes to more personal subjects, however, many people pay therapists just to have someone listen to them express their feelings—if they talk about them at all. Despite the ability to be in constant contact with others, the art of dialogue is dying. The concept of connecting intimately through conversation—the process of sharing meaningful thoughts and deep feelings—is almost lost except in the professional counseling realm.

4. *Self-esteem has reached an unbearable stage.* At any given moment we have more than 100 billion neurons shouting that we are unique— that no one occupies the stage of our lives exactly as we do. But the fashion industry's influence and the prevalence of plastic surgery and cosmetic medicine—which alter our originality and make us appear more like "everyone else"—have all increased. Looking better was supposed to make us feel better and live better, yet the collective self-esteem of the human race continues to worsen. The dictatorship of beauty in modern society has destroyed self-image to the point that

there are approximately 50 million people around the world suffering from anorexia nervosa—a statistic that vividly illustrates how severe the current crisis of self-esteem is.

5. *Thinkers are dwindling.* We have raised a generation of students who don't know how to think. Their minds are filled with cheap thoughts and ideas instead. Young people are learning to imitate instead of interact, to think carelessly instead of critically. And the consequences of that will be felt for centuries to come unless each generation begins to practice and live by the principles detailed in this book.

6. *Psychological health is deteriorating.* Despite the advances in medicine, psychology, and psychiatry, people aren't becoming collectively healthier—anxiety and stress are still the norm, while living a tranquil and relaxed life is practically unheard-of. The sciences of the psyche have not helped as much as we'd expect either. They've focused on treatment and not prevention. Yet nothing is more scientifically unjust than to wait until the mind is diseased and then treat it.

## Multi-Focal Psychology

Lest anyone consider me a pessimist, let me clarify: I seek to be a realist—I'm a psychiatrist who loves life and continuously writes about what I observe and analyze. But I am also a therapist and researcher who wants to contribute to the quality of life of my patients and society at large. What you will read in this book is my attempt to come to grips with the deteriorating state of human experience and offer a strategy that will reverse the six trends I have just cited; a program that will promote psychological health among individuals and a better society in general. How does this work?

When our thinking is done "correctly," it can produce in us the quality of life we want. The latest research, such as *The Mindful Brain* by Dan Siegel, *The Field* and *The Intention Experiment* by Lynne McTaggart, *Multiple Intelligences* by Howard Gardner, *The Biology of Belief* by Bruce Lipton, and the works of Bernard Baars—especially *Cognition, Brain, and*

*Consciousness*—confirms again and again that this is true. Even the success of Rhonda Byrne's *The Secret*, with its popular positive psychology that has attracted millions, shows that people are realizing we do become what we think. However, more is needed. As we say in my country of Brazil, "We need to work more and to walk more."

The mind has unlimited power, but with its secrets hidden and its "tools" underutilized, it is often misused and misunderstood. What are the secrets and tools of the intellect that we need to improve our psychological health? That is the subject of this book. Its foundation is my Multi-Focal Psychology theory,[1] which I developed over the course of twenty years and on which I have written more than three thousand pages, including twenty books. In essence, this theory investigates the four primary processes of the human psyche, or mind: (1) the construction of thoughts, (2) the transformation of emotions, (3) the forming of consciousness and the foundations of "self," and (4) the role of memory and the forming of the existential story of one's personality.

The term *multi-focal* means that the theory integrates the many different ways the mind works to direct our actions and to develop personality. The theory focuses not just on thoughts *but on how thoughts are constructed—what is actually going on when we "think."* For example, Multi-Focal Psychology asks: What is the nature of thought? How do we build chains of ideas and mental images? How do we develop the awareness that we are unique? How do emotions transform themselves in fractions of a second? What are the links between thoughts and emotions? How is the story of our life organized and used within the memory? Getting behind thoughts to their actual origin allows new levels of insight into the human experience.

Over and above everything else, though, Multi-Focal Psychology recognizes that the human act of thinking—building a thought in a nanosecond out of the billions of pieces of information stored in memory—is the greatest wonder known to mankind. It's a wonder—and a world—we need to access more fully.

# A Revolutionary Program

Because the processes of Multi-Focal Psychology are foundational to the way the human mind works, this theory does not compete with other theories but can supplement them instead. Thus you will find the content of this book helpful no matter what psychological systems or practices you adhere to in your day-to-day life.

This book is not an explanation of Multi-Focal theory, however, but is instead an application of its principles, which combine the disciplines of education, psychology, philosophy, psychiatry, and sociology. Applying these principles can help you harness the unlimited power of your mind, which will lead you to gain the happiness you seek and achieve the extraordinary quality of life that you desire.

However, we do need to understand certain aspects of our complex mind in order to gain the knowledge and the courage to take control of our lives, to perform at our peak, and to thus achieve the quality of life we want. We need to understand that each human being has the potential to develop a mind that thinks correctly—one that is amazing, extraordinary, powerful, competent, vigorous, influential, remarkable, creative, humble, secure, tranquil, imaginative, free, enterprising, determined, motivated, full of insight, inspired, illuminated, and visionary. When we don't think correctly, it's not because our memory has failed us—as people often believe—but that certain central functions of the mind have been misused and perhaps even misunderstood. Yet inside each of us are the tools and secrets we need—what I call Think Correctly "principles"—and these will be explored in each chapter of this book. At the end of each chapter there will be application questions and helpful reminders, plus remarkable stories from real people who demonstrate these principles, showing you that everyone is capable of thinking correctly.

This book is not intended to replace necessary psychiatric and psychological treatments, but it can complement them. The more important functions of the principles presented here include improving specific areas of the mind to prevent psychological disorders, to help form thinkers and leaders, to expand creativity and pleasure, and to overcome loneliness and low self-esteem.

By understanding how the mind processes information, you will learn how to respond skillfully to life instead of reacting dangerously to stress, frustration, and loss. Thinking correctly allows you to transform information into knowledge, knowledge into experience, and experience into the shaping of your mind. When you learn to think correctly, you can become the person you want to be.

## Three Ways to Read This Book

There are three ways to profit from this book, listed below in increasing order of effectiveness:

1. Read it as you would any other book, with a view to increasing your intelligence and wisdom.
2. Read one chapter per week, with a view toward incorporating and living each principle, and then review the principles continually as a lifelong program for change.
3. Work through the twelve principles (one per week) as part of a small group, benefiting from the experiences and interactions of others and the synergy that results. In appendix B you will see how to form and facilitate these groups in your company, university, family, or religious community. At the end of each chapter, I've included important thoughts to use to discuss in the group and to reflect on personally.

## A Model of Thinking Correctly

There is one more element to this book. Whether you're creating a new building, a new car, or a new life, every new development needs a model to go by. Likewise, we need a model in the psychological world by which to measure our own development toward maturity.

I once did a thorough study of a number of history's greatest men — Moses, Buddha, Mohammed, Confucius, Socrates, Plato, Freud, Einstein, and Jesus of Nazareth. In the end, I was so taken by Jesus' psychological health that it jarred me out of my skepticism about him. I was one of the best atheists on this earth, perhaps more firm in my belief in atheism than Marx, Nietzsche, Sartre, and Diderot. But when I used Multi-Focal Psychology to study Jesus' personality detail by detail, I was surprised, perplexed, and shocked by what I found.

I came to understand that it is impossible for human intellect to make up a person with his characteristics, for never has anyone led others so well as a result of first leading himself to the highest reaches of life. He was a nonconformist in the best sense of the word, refusing to adopt the fears and neuroses of the world in which he lived. Of all the accounts of individual men and women we have from history, it is my professional psychiatric opinion that no person has modeled the kind of rich life we need better than him. Unfortunately, history has focused almost exclusively on Jesus' divinity to the exclusion of his humanity.

However, from my scientific standpoint, Jesus the man had a spectacular ability to think correctly. His creativity was remarkable, his capacity to manage his thoughts in the face of tension was wonderful, and his ability to protect his emotions was unprecedented. He had every reason to be sad, depressed, and anxious, but he was happy, tranquil, and secure. And his model as a human being is something we will examine in this book.

Let me emphasize that I am not talking about him from a religious perspective but from a psychological, psychiatric, philosophical, and pedagogical context. This book respects all people, including atheists. However, I believe no one has influenced history more than Jesus. This book will use the way he "thought correctly" as a model for all of us.

## It's Your Choice

My professional goals in life are to democratize and popularize science and its findings—to share with as many people as possible the discoveries that can lead to an enhanced quality of life. My desire is that all people—regardless of race, religion, social status, or cultural background—learn to manage their thoughts and lives and invest deeply in themselves. Each person is a complex world unto himself. Each individual can have a leading role—or be a key "actor" (participant)—in the theater of human experience. It's my desire that you fulfill your role in this life with maximum effect and impact.

When it comes to making the most of your thinking mind, imagine this: there are two ways to stay warm in life—build a fire with dry wood or plant seeds that will ultimately provide wood for a lifetime. Which do you prefer? Most people opt for immediate comfort using available resources, which in our case would be those resources—and even distractions—provided by modern culture. But such resources are quickly consumed and provide no lasting change.

This book instead presents twelve "seeds"—twelve Think Correctly principles. Planting seeds, while harder and slower, yields resources that provide permanent, ongoing comfort and change. When these fantastic seeds flourish, the most beautiful forest appears. What will be the result? You will always have wood to warm yourself and those you love. You will never be the same again, and neither will society. Why not make a difference in the world and participate in this dream?

Thousands of people—including doctors, psychologists, teachers, spiritual leaders, employers, parents, and teenagers—have used the principles of the Think Correctly program. They've changed their lives and developed their intellects. Now it is time for you to discover what they have discovered: that your mind really is extraordinarily beautiful and powerful, and able to transform your entire quality of life.

Dr. Augusto Cury
USA
Winter 2008

## CHAPTER ONE

*Principle #1:*

# Be the Author of Your Own Story

In summary form, here is what it means to be the author of your own story:

1. Recognize the greatness of life and the fascinating story inscribed in your memory.
2. Establish and follow clear goals.
3. Make choices to reach your goals.
4. Make decisions and correct poor choices.
5. Recognize your limits, flaws, and psychological weaknesses.
6. Don't give up on life when facing difficulties.
7. Be transparent and honest.
8. Be self-controlled.
9. Learn to lead yourself before trying to lead others.
10. Train your mind to live out all twelve Think Correctly principles.

## Life: Grand, Beautiful, and Indefinable

Have you ever known someone who was very accomplished in his career or very gifted at some skill but whose ability to manage his mind and emotions was almost nonexistent? Have you known anyone who was a public success but whose personal life—her thoughts, private actions, and relationships—was in shambles? Have you ever met someone who does what he does only because he has life and breath in him, not because he understands a greater possibility? Someone who has not yet discovered the extraordinary potential of his mind or his ability to think correctly and make life happen *for* him rather than *to* him?

If so, then you've likely met someone who has not learned Think Correctly Principle #1: *Be the author of your own story.*

In fact, at this very moment there are executives managing companies, public servants running cities, and pilots flying planes with great success, but many of them are defeated by bad moods, hypochondria, anxiety, and irritability. They are giants in society, and perhaps even in industry, but fragile beings within themselves. They are extremely capable when controlling the external world, but they lack wisdom to manage the internal universe of their minds; their fears, anxieties, and preoccupations are always in danger of taking over.

Their problems are not necessarily due to arrogance or egocentricity. Sometimes people with an unhealthy self are among the most affectionate and kind people you'll ever meet. But they don't value themselves or put time into themselves. They know how to invest in material things, but they don't know how to invest in developing their minds so that they experience the wonderful thoughts and emotions that accompany a healthy life.

The truth is, if the internal self is ill, then the development of one's personality will be compromised: the psyche will have no shelter, the emotions will be a no-man's land, and the ability to make decisions will fluctuate. Case in point: I was once giving a lecture on the process of developing the self and its effect on the psyche. One participant stood up and humbly said to the audience, "I spent my life never knowing that I had a 'self,' or even that this 'self' was supposed to manage and organize my thoughts and emotions so that I wouldn't become a victim of them!"

Although this man had an excellent academic background and was a dominant force in management, he had no basic information about how he worked psychologically! He was a respected executive in the outside world but was only beginning to understand that he was a weak leader of the main "corporation" for which he was responsible: his own mind.

He suffered intensely because he hadn't learned how to recycle his fears, rethink his impulses, and remove the power from his pessimistic thoughts—things we'll discuss in this book. He had money, professional success, and social prestige, but he felt miserable in the only place where being poor is inadmissible: within his own being. He created mental and emotional upheaval for himself—what I call "psychological earthquakes"—without knowing it, and they always shook him. He was a stranger to himself, and his mind was constantly anxious. As a result, he had difficulty making decisions and sticking with them.

Unfortunately, he was not alone. We all know adults who act like children or adolescents. They have not developed minds that will think correctly and produce the extraordinary life they're capable of. Thus, their stories are being written by everyone except themselves, and it is to their detriment.

Let me explain. Our "individual story," as I call it, is archived in our memory and is our personality's lifetime accumulation of secrets—the events and influences that have shaped us. Every single person and event in our lives has made a contribution, consciously or not, to who we are today. Each of us accumulates billions of new thoughts, perceptions, and influences each year just by going about our lives. Along with our genetic code, these are what shape us. However, what many people fail to realize is that we have a life-changing choice in this area: we can be passive about these thoughts and influences—passive about the construction of our lives—and let everything and everyone shape the story but us, or we can use the powers of our mind to become the authors as well as the active participants, the "actors."

And this power extends even to our genetic code. A brand-new branch of science called *epigenetics*—control of genes from outside the cell—promises a revolution in health and happiness. Our DNA does not determine our destiny to the degree we once thought. Extensive new scientific research shows that many genes are being turned on and off— every day—by our beliefs, feelings, and attitudes. Every thought we think ripples throughout our body, affecting our immune system, brain, and hormones.

To put it metaphorically, life is a great book. A mature, healthy person is one who recognizes it is her responsibility to write the text, line after line, page after page, year after year. A person who thinks correctly combines vision and creativity to write happiness in this book from life's good moments and to write wisdom and humility from the bad moments.

When you do this day by day, you begin to expand specific areas of your mind so that it gradually transforms from ordinary to brilliant. So that it gradually becomes not only competent, humble, secure, and tranquil but also more enterprising, determined, and full of insight.

## Where Do We Start?

Humans are complex beings—the most complex on the planet— due to our unique ability to think and remember. Just consider the complicated web of thoughts, emotions, and memories that cross your mind in the course of a single day—thousands of them! The goal of this book is to deepen your appreciation of your own amazing complexity and beauty so that you can better utilize your potential, or *think correctly*, and make wonderful things happen. It is also intended to help you extend that appreciation to others, which goes against human nature.

The history of the human race is the history of people "depreciating," rather than appreciating, others. Throughout the centuries we have discriminated against others and thus divided ourselves rather than calling upon our power to think and to unite. Too many times we have failed to recognize that we are all equal. In the first place, we are not Christians, Jews, and Muslims; Brazilian and Chinese; Socialist and Democrat. We are all human beings. Yes, we have cultural, intellectual, and genetic differences, but we are alike in far more ways than we are different. And the ways we are different tend to be superficial. A mind that thinks correctly loves people and understands that discrimination is unintelligent and inhumane—that it negates the very reality that should give us the power to create a quality of life that we can enjoy.

Anyone who doesn't appreciate the beauty and diversity of the human species will never achieve a high quality of life and will never gain true wisdom or happiness. Every human being is a world unto himself, waiting to be explored—a story to be understood and told, a land to be cultivated. And the human mind is a treasure to be unveiled. Yet the fact that we value Hollywood celebrities above "ordinary" people is evidence of our failure to grasp this truth.

To be the author of our own story, we have to realize that, first of all, for ourselves and also for every human who shares this planet with us, we each have a story to tell, a song to sing, a canvas to paint—not just the "celebrities" among us. That is one reason I rarely give interviews in my country: I don't warrant the attention because I am not better than anyone else. Some people want to make it seem as if my intellect is superior, but it's not. I have simply invested a lot of time developing my mind, which anyone else can do too. In addition, I am fully aware that in a short time, just like any other mortal, the wonder of my earthly existence will end in the silence of a grave. What will I take with me? What will you take? What is the value of status, fame, and social prestige at that mysterious moment when life as we've known it ends?

Truly, the best pleasures and the greatest wonders in this life are the quieter ones that often go unnoticed but that are available to us all. We are convinced that what really makes us happy are our circumstances, but if we were thinking correctly, we'd realize this is not the case.

Not long ago, a blind man sat next to me on a plane. I asked him about his blindness, and he told me about its physiological aspects. Because of his articulate explanation, I asked him if he was a doctor. He said no, he was a psychotherapist who conducted training programs for hundreds of professionals throughout the country. Then he asked me my name. "Augusto," I said.

He frowned. "Are you not Augusto Cury?"

Embarrassed, and without understanding the reason for his question, I admitted that I was. He then handed me the headphones to his CD player. One of my audio books was playing. He went on to explain that he had just given a lecture on several of my ideas.

As we exchanged a number of experiences, we mutually marveled at how life gains another dimension when people see that it's a wonder we just can't afford to miss. This man's blindness had not prevented him from loving life, loving others, and investing in himself. And my "celebrity" had not made me immune to the need for the same priorities and outlook on life. Thus, to apply Principle #1—Be the author of your own story—you must (1) become a person who acknowledges your great uniqueness and complexity as well as that of others. You must also (2) be someone who never diminishes yourself with feelings of inferiority or self-pity. This is likely to happen when we compare ourselves to other people, so don't go there. Acknowledging your equality with others is key. Finally, (3) you must learn to become your own leader.

## Leading Ourselves

I define "self" as that which represents our critical conscience, our conscious will, and our capacity to decide. The self is our identity—our ability to analyze situations, think critically, make choices, exercise our free will, course-correct, establish goals, manage emotions, and govern thoughts. For the purposes of this book, apart from the discussions of developmental psychology, I will generally use more common terms (such as "I," "he" or "she," and "you") to indicate the self, as this is how the psychological definition of *self* is popularly understood.

As we researchers of psychology describe it, the self is "actualized" early in an infant's life as he begins to recognize himself as separate from others—especially separate from his nursing mother. This is expressed as the infant begins to reach, to demand, to enjoy, to cry—all the actions that gradually reflect the thinking process that is taking place. By adolescence the self should be well-founded, and by adulthood it should be prepared to exercise mature leadership, or management, of ourselves.

This doesn't mean that we will never have "unauthorized" thoughts and emotions. We will discover in future chapters that one of the most complex abilities of the human mind is just that: to produce thoughts and feelings that occur on their own, without our permission or invitation. Unfortunately, these thoughts that "pop into our minds" often destroy our tranquillity, but the fact that they occur does not mean a person is not leading himself.

An unhealthy and immature person—the one who is not leading himself as a way of life—will manifest that by being indecisive, insecure, unstable, anxious, and enslaved by destructive thoughts and emotions. Educated and powerful people can have an unhealthy self and assume no internal leadership just like anyone else. They may be able to run giant corporations or even nations but be unable to resolve inner problems and internal conflicts. Thinking correctly requires the development of a healthy self.

## Writing Your Story

In this book I will often refer to our lives as taking place "in the theater of" or "on the stage of" our minds. What I mean is, we play out what we think and how we think before a watching "audience" of friends, family, and coworkers. Imagine the mind as a huge theater with an empty stage. Too many people live their lives in the audience rather than on the stage. They passively watch their own lives—their psychological dramas and conflicts—being played out, believing they are powerless to write the script or direct the actors. Writing one's own story means leaving the audience, going onto the stage, and directing the action of one's life, scene after scene.

Some psychology theories say it is impossible to change the personality you're born with and begin to assume control of the course of your life, but this is scientifically incorrect. Shaping children is easier, of course, because their minds are younger and less formed. But adults at any age can begin to author their own stories and experience significant changes. And it all starts with our minds.

I'll elaborate on this in the next chapter, but we are thinking all the time, and every single thought—conscious or not—affects us and shapes us for good or for ill. That means we are changing all the time too—whether we work at it or not! However, because we live in a world filled with negative, disturbing images, it is easy to be changed more for ill than for good. Especially if we're not developing our minds and filtering what comes our way.

Despite the human mind being the most beautiful organism in all of nature, it easily acquires "conflict"—inferiority complexes, timidity, phobias, depression, obsessions, panic syndrome, psychosomatic illnesses, rigidity, perfectionism, insecurity, impulsivity, excessive concerns with the future and with one's social image (and the list goes on)—especially when we don't assume responsibility for what happens within us. Authoring our own story means taking control of that which fills our minds and influences us, so as to make the changes positive instead of negative. It means intervening to deflect negative influences and keep them from shaping our personality.

This is not to say that flexible people don't have their moments of impatience, or calm people their moments of anxiety, or clear-thinking people their moments of incoherence. We all need help in some area of our personality. But only when people become equipped to take charge of the ongoing drama being played out in the theater of the mind will they find the quality of life they seek. And as individuals become the authors of their own stories, so will societies begin to write higher-quality stories as well.

## How Our Model of Thinking Correctly Authored His Own Story

Jesus of Nazareth authored his own story. He was completely focused on his purpose in life and would allow nothing to keep him from accomplishing it.

In a passage in the Old Testament of the Bible there is a phrase that describes this attitude. Even in the midst of suffering, says the writer: "[I have] set my face like flint, and I know I will not be put to shame."[1]

That's how Jesus was. Suffering and hardship were not enough to keep him from his appointed mission. Like flint—one of the hardest minerals known—he set his face toward his objective.

Neither did our model allow the conventions of his time to influence who he was. He is particularly remembered as one who associated with the outcasts of his society. The poor, the diseased, the immoral, the hated—all found a friend in Jesus.

To associate with the dregs of society meant to invite the same scorn and persecution upon himself that was received by those with whom he associated. But Jesus willingly stood against the ridicule that was heaped upon him, for the sake of being true to the life story that he was writing. He had the ability to see the diamond hidden in the lump of coal, the gold concealed in the ore. Jesus' story was redemptive in nature, and he refused to let external influences push him off that story line. He believed all people were redeemable and reached out to them without fail.

A person with an ordinary mind rejects people who have a deplorable social image, but a person who thinks correctly acts differently. He invests in them. My psychological analysis of Jesus' personality convinces me that his humanity was more revolutionary, generous, and excellent than that of the great thinkers such as Rousseau, Voltaire, Marx, Jung, Skinner, Sartre, Pasteur, or Darwin. Jesus believed that every individual has great value and deserves respect. He knew that although people do make poor decisions and suffer the consequences, the quality of their lives can still be increased.

Because love was the main theme of Jesus' story, he was able to look beneath the surface of a person's life and, using extraordinary wisdom and discernment, know what was going on inside them. He "knew" that he was being persecuted out of envy;[2] he "knew" what religious leaders thought about his life;[3] he "knew" the impulsive and sometimes fickle nature of man;[4] he "knew" the difference between what seemed true on the outside and what was true on the inside of a person. And thus he was not surprised by anything that happened to him.

It was this knowledge that also prevented him from reacting defensively or angrily toward others. He knew where people were coming from, as we would say today. He knew the damage people had suffered in their lives—their fears, suspicions, apprehensions, and jealousies. His story line was strong enough not to be blown off course by the strong winds of others' weaknesses.

Achieving a quality of life as high as Jesus' will mean being in control of your own story, regardless of how adamantly others try to rewrite it.

## Leading Oneself in the Midst of Stress

Jesus' popularity among the common people was a threat to the influential leaders of his day. Their jealousy and hatred ran deep. In order to get rid of him on legitimate grounds, they continually tried to entrap him—to find him guilty of religious crimes that even the crowds and commoners could not argue with.

One of their most despicable attempts at entrapment was to bring to Jesus a woman who'd been caught in the act of adultery. According to Jewish religious law, she should have been stoned to death. Knowing of Jesus' compassion toward people who had failed in life, the religious leaders asked him what should be done with the woman. They hoped he would say, "Release her"—violating the law—causing the crowd to turn against him. The crowd would then likely stone Jesus to death along with the woman.

On the other hand, if Jesus said, "She must be put to death," he would be going against his own story line of forgiveness. I have to give the religious leaders credit for crafting a brilliant plot—one seemingly leaving no escape route. Imagine being in the crowd as the issue was raised. Feel the tension shared by all, awaiting the teacher's response.

What would you have done? What is your normal reaction when you feel trapped, betrayed, cornered, or unjustly treated? What would you do if everything you had worked for was about to be ruined by others? If someone jerked the pen out of your hand and said, "I'll write your story from here on"?

Our inclination is to react impulsively and irrationally. Too often we say and do things we later regret because fear, anger, and anxiety consume us. Out of our internal archives come memories of similar incidents in the past and how painful they were. Our defenses kick in and we lose control, forfeiting our own story lines.

The situation was ripe for Jesus to respond in the same way. He was being trapped and set up for failure—perhaps death—by a group of angry, insecure, jealous, power-hungry men. But instead of reacting as they hoped, he did what he so often did—that which no one would have anticipated: he used the tool of silence.

Jesus demonstrated a powerful principle: in circumstances where no one is thinking, the best answer is to give no answer at all.

In moments of stress it is often during the first thirty seconds that we make our gravest mistakes. It is during those initial, highly charged moments that we say and do things we later regret. Jesus chose to say nothing. He withdrew into himself, rose above his emotions, and gained control of his own story. And when he did, he seized the ability to lead himself out of that life-threatening situation.

Jesus' first movement, according to the Gospel of John, was to bend down and begin to write in the sand. This unexpected act on his part put his accusers on the defensive. They didn't have the wisdom to know how to respond to Jesus' actions, and thus they continued to question him while he was squatting and writing[5]—another indication of their insecurity. (How often do we rant and rave, engaging in ad hominem attacks, when we are out of reasonable things to say?) Only a person like Jesus, a person thinking correctly, can find a place of rest in the midst of a battle. His serene demeanor and controlled behavior still astonish those of us who study human behavior.

## Out of the Audience, Onto the Stage

The complex and mysterious book called the Bible does not tell us what Jesus wrote in the sand. Perhaps he was writing about tolerance and compassion—qualities very important for strong relationships but often underdeveloped in our ordinary minds. But what Jesus did next further confirmed that, even in the midst of a terrible attack, it is possible to be the author of one's own story.

Jesus was about to give his attackers an opportunity to regain control over the story of their own lives. Up to that point they had been driven by jealousy and insecurity. They were willing to sacrifice the life of a needy woman in order to destroy a man they saw as a rival, a competitor, in their sphere of power and influence. But Jesus offered them a chance at a higher quality of life. He invited them to leave the audience (remember: the audience is the place of no control, the place of passivity, the place where we watch others write the stories of our lives) and come up on the stage with him and write a new chapter in their personal stories.

Jesus stood up from where he had been writing and said, "If any one of you is without sin [wrongdoing, failure, hypocrisy], let him be the first to throw a stone at her."[6] He actually invited them to stone the woman to death! But under entirely different circumstances. They would have to stop and evaluate their own lives before choosing how to respond to her.

In this, Jesus gave the accusers the opportunity to exercise one of the most extraordinary and powerful functions of the human mind: empathy—putting oneself in the place of another before acting. No other creature on the planet has the power to do this. No lioness on the plains of the Serengeti ever stops to think, *I wonder how that young antelope will feel when I lock my jaws around its neck. I wonder how its mother will feel when I tear apart the fruit of her womb.* Only human beings have the psychological and intellectual ability to empathize.

When Jesus invited the religious leaders onto the stage with him, he gave them the opportunity to examine their own frailties and failures, to turn the page and write a new chapter in their stories. For a brief moment (we see later that their change of heart was only temporary) they decided not to play victim to fear, jealousy, and prejudice. They walked away from what might have been the scene of a double murder.

By maintaining authorship of his own story, Jesus brought a moment of sanity to an out-of-control situation.

How many times in history has a lynch mob been turned away by the voice of wisdom and reason? How many times has a suicide bomber decided to put aside irrational hatred and unstrap the bombs from his body? The ability to defuse bombs and disarm attackers is within human potential—Jesus proved it. But how often do we see it done in our world? How often have you done it in yours?

## Following Our Model

An influential and competent mind understands that the best way to disarm an aggressor is with the unexpected. Aggressors are prepared for the expected, the predictable—force, retaliation, argument—but not for the unanticipated. Silence, surprise, a compliment, a question, an attitude of serenity or kindness—there are many ways to tip the balance in favor of a peaceful resolution.

Even Jesus' disciples had to learn to respond as he did. Had they been in his position, they likely would have insisted the woman be stoned. On one occasion when his disciples were rebuffed by a rival religious group, they asked their teacher, "Lord, do you want us to call fire down from heaven to destroy them?"[7] Instead of correcting the people who had attacked his disciples, Jesus corrected his disciples! They were the ones who lost control, who put themselves back into the audience while their memories of rival bitterness drove them to seek destructive behavior. It was their responsibility to develop their own stories; to be the authors of their own lives.

Jesus' disciples needed to learn, as do we, that the greatest leader is the one who writes his own story, the one who stays on the stage as the active actor-director, not the one who retreats into the audience as a passive observer. As we see later in the New Testament, Jesus' disciples appear to have learned well from the model of correct thinking.

If we humans practiced only 10 percent of the tools and principles demonstrated by Jesus' correctly thinking mind, we would see headline issues such as war, violence, predatory competition, discrimination, hatred, selfish ambition, and social crises relegated to the pages of the dictionary. Gandhi is reported to have said to Lord Irwin of India, "When your country and mine shall get together on the teachings laid down by Christ in this Sermon on the Mount, we shall have solved the problems, not only of our countries, but those of the whole world."

---

*Thinking Correctly to Be the Author of Your Own Story:*
## My own experience with depression

Human existence is a complex labyrinth to tread. One moment we're smiling, and the next, we're crying. We are applauded during one occasion and forgotten the next. In one season we're unbeatable, and in the next season we're constantly defeated.

None of us can control all the factors that comprise a life or be prepared for everything that happens. We barely control the variables that involve us personally, such as the use of our time or abilities; in our jobs and our homes and at school, others influence even those things. In fact, life eventually teaches us that the process of living is neither predictable nor stable. That's why it has been said that "one thing is for sure: everything is unsure."

So being the author of our own stories doesn't mean that we're invincible, or that we are never caught by surprise, or that our lives are devoid of crises. No! It means that we overcome the surprises as well as our psychological upheavals with dignity, writing the most important texts of our personalities during our journey. I have taken this journey myself, flaws, mistakes, and all.

So that you know this book is born of reality, I will demonstrate how I applied the first principle of thinking correctly to my own story during a dramatic depressive crisis I went through while I was still in medical school.

Many people are afraid of being in touch with themselves and telling their stories. They suffocate their pain under a cloak of timidity and insecurity. We like to talk about our successes, but we are silent about our failures. In this text I will do the opposite.

My med school classmates saw me as a secure person. Depression was the last thing that people expected I'd struggle with. I was sociable, fearless, and in love with life. But I was also a hypersensitive person who didn't realize it. Problems, losses, and frustrations easily invaded my emotions. And though I didn't know how to protect my mind and emotions, I typically bounced back.

Because of genetic influences, however (my mother, who was a wonderful person, suffered with chronic depression), and without any knowledge of how to write my own story or protect myself internally when faced with stressful circumstances, I eventually went through the confusing valley of depression. I was heading into my third year of medical school.

I tried to hide my crisis from my friends; like many people, I was afraid of being misunderstood and socially excluded, so I cried dry tears—silent on the outside but shouting on the inside. Can you relate? I took unnecessary risks, unaware of what depression was, what its causes or consequences were—unaware that I was even suffering from it or that it should be treated. Now, of course, I understand that its causes aren't always evident; they may lie within the brain's metabolism, in pessimistic thoughts, in disturbing mental images and memories, or in concrete circumstances. But back then, I couldn't find a legitimate reason for my feelings or actions, which left me at a greater loss. I only knew that I had lost all pleasure in living, and I felt a deep sadness and a tightness in my chest.

My mind was restless; my thoughts were tense and negative. I had insomnia, and I had lost my appetite. No wonder I woke up feeling tired! I dragged my body through each day with no motivation and with as little social contact as possible. Joy had dissipated from my life like drops of dew absorbed by the first rays of sunshine on a summer morning.

Though my friends were near, I couldn't move myself to reach out to them. Nothing cheered me up; nothing enchanted me. If I had been given the entire world, I still would have felt like the poorest of men. If people had applauded me, I still would have considered myself the most anonymous of human beings. I was isolated within myself, a victim of the most penetrating and inexplicable loneliness I've ever known.

Many weeks went by, and I grew progressively more fragile. If I had been told about psychological illnesses and that it's all right to get help, I would have seen a psychiatrist. But even in medical schools at that time, there was a lot of prejudice in this area. So I continued to experience my pain like a spectator watching a horror movie, a spectator incapable of changing the scenes, who could only cover his eyes or leave the theater. My dilemma was this: How could I close my eyes to myself? How could I escape from the monsters that were haunting my emotions? It was as if I had been programmed to suffer.

But then I had an insight—one moment of thinking correctly that ended up being a turning point. Even though my internal self was not well formed and I had not begun to develop my mind, I managed to realize, *Either I'll be the victim of my suffering, or I will face it and try to have victory over it.* I didn't know how to penetrate inside myself, but I had to do it, for in psychic battles there are no two winners. If the self is intimidated, it loses. It's that simple. The mind becomes ill every time it doesn't act in its own favor.

A creative intuition blossomed from that insight, and I decided to rise out of my inertia and fight my worst enemy. And what enemy was that? The one that slept in my inner world. I decided to, in essence, engage my inner leader and take charge of my life.

Once I discovered that I even had this choice and then exercised the choice to be in charge, I stopped being a victim of my depression and started taking my first steps toward authoring my own story.

Step one was to stop wasting energy in complaining and asking, "Why me?"

Step two was to be honest with myself and recognize my emotional pain and psychological conflict.

Step three was to go inside myself and not only recognize what I was feeling but immerse myself in the waters of emotion, letting myself experience the depths of those emotions, whatever they were.

Step four was to "map" my struggle through the art of self-observation and journaling, discovering the dimensions of my pain, how it affected me, how it appeared, to what causes it was linked, and what its roots were.

Step five was to disagree with my passive attitude and give up my tendency to put my life on autopilot.

Step six was to learn to "doubt" and "criticize" my own depression.

We'll discuss these ideas in later chapters, but during my internal storm, I wrote numerous pages every day containing my observations and insights—an internal journal if you will. In a short time I had hundreds of pages. The art of internalizing—going inside myself and observing, deducting, inducting, and appropriately criticizing and doubting (which I'll explain in chapter 2)—was the foundation that led me to develop the Think Correctly principles detailed in this book.

And the outcome? As I took time every day to be introspective and determine the size of the monster that haunted me, evaluating its causes and its potential, I realized that this monster was smaller than I had imagined—and that I was stronger than I thought. I realized that I could make choices. And I chose to be free.

During my emotional crisis, amid all of the other questions I asked and explored, I made discoveries in two psychotherapeutic areas: analytical and cognitive-behavioral. They're frequently separated in treatment, but I intuitively joined them and thus was able not only to penetrate the causes of my psychological desert but also to act on its symptoms.

In a few weeks my mind was once again flourishing like a field of sunflowers in a tropical plain. Years later, once I had become a psychiatrist, I began to apply this technique with my patients. I'll tell you the stories of some of these patients in the following chapters.

As I became the author of my own story, I learned that *pain either strengthens us or destroys us*. I learned that, depending on the path we take, we might become our own greatest enemies. But we are also capable of becoming our own heroes if we think correctly and write our stories carefully.

It will take learning that life is worth living even when the world comes crashing down on us, and that the secrets of a rich and healthy mind are hidden away where the eyes cannot see. But at all times, the story line is within our grasp.

## SUGGESTED TOPICS FOR REFLECTION AND DISCUSSION

1. Your life is a unique gem in the treasure of existence: we each have a rich story. Have you invested in the quality of your life, or have you been passive about it?
2. All discrimination is unintelligent. Have you felt or do you feel inferior to other people? What is the true value you give your life and the people who surround you?
3. Empowering your inner leader means making conscious decisions that will benefit you. What disturbs you the most in the theater of your mind? What decisions have you postponed in your life?
4. A fragile person is not the author of his story and does not manage his thoughts or emotions. Are you irritable and anxious? Impulsive and intolerant? Do you demand too much of yourself? Do you demand too much of others? What personality characteristics would you like to overcome?
5. Love was the foundation of Jesus' wisdom. How much do you love life and other people?
6. Jesus used silence to call up his inner leader, and thus he was able to think before he acted. Do you use silence in tense situations? Are you

able to have self-control and surprise your coworkers and family with your response when they disappoint you?

## EXERCISES AND REMINDERS FOR DAILY PRACTICE

1. Referencing the characteristics of Principle #1—"Be the author of your own story"—that were described at the beginning of this chapter, journal about which qualities you need to develop.
2. List in your journal the decisions that you have postponed that need to be made.
3. Practice learning how to think before reacting. Learn to use the tool of silence when tension with others arises.
4. When every human being builds a thought, he is a great artist, even if he lives in anonymity. Never feel inferior to other people.
5. Never give up on the people you love, and never give up on yourself.
6. Do not be enslaved by your conflicts. Know what you want for your life. Practice leaving the audience each day, going onto the stage of your mind, and being your own director as well as the main actor. Free up your inner leader to do what it does best.
7. Face your pain, difficulties, anguish, sad moods, and negative thoughts with dignity. Do not fear your psychological misery, and do not fear being the author of your own story.

## CHAPTER TWO

*Principle #2:*

# Direct Your Thoughts

The frenetic pace of modern society encourages frenetic think-ing. Living in a world of constant sound bites and ever-changing visual images forces our minds to try and keep pace. Instead of managing our thoughts, we feel we do well just to keep up with them. But to think correctly, more is required.

Here are eight characteristics of a person who manages his or her thoughts:

1. Decides to become the lead actor in the theater of the mind, to leave the audience and become the director of life's script
2. Is free to think but not a slave to thoughts; is the master, not the servant, of thoughts
3. Governs thoughts—allowing quality thoughts to thrive but blocking thoughts that hinder development and debilitate mental health
4. Exercises dominance over thoughts that produce psychological disorders
5. Exercises leadership of the self to become a person of influence

6. Resists the temptation to be a passive spectator of negative ideas, fears, anguish, and anxiety
7. Refuses to fixate on past or future problems
8. Has a relaxed, tranquil mind instead of an agitated life

## A Critical Step

This particular principle of how to think correctly—"Direct Your Thoughts"—is one of the most important pillars of a healthy life, since everything we are or will become has its origin in the mind.

As we've all experienced, our thoughts can either be a source of pleasure or a source of pain. The person who learns to manage his thoughts every day develops one of the most critical areas of his mind and becomes all the more powerful for having taken charge of what most people consider an impossible territory to conquer. However, as we will see in this chapter, our thoughts can be mastered. And this will put us one step closer to achieving the quality of life we desire.

## I Think, Therefore I Am

Thinking is a spontaneous and inevitable human activity. Within the human mind there is an uninterrupted psychic show that doesn't stop even when we sleep (we call the nighttime version "dreams"). These shows, where we construct fantasies, characters, and complex scenarios, can sometimes disturb us enough to haunt us, because we're not sure if they reveal something about us that we're not aware of on a conscious level. But what most people don't know is that our minds are constantly flowing with thoughts, awake or asleep. As long as you're alive, you will have that thought-stream night and day. Inevitably, if the conscious "self"—which as I've said represents the will, the capacity to choose, and the power of self-determination—doesn't produce thoughts, the unconscious will. Automatically. It's that simple.

This is exactly where a mind that thinks correctly kicks into high gear. To live by Principle #2—to direct your thoughts—means to produce thoughts on a conscious level rather than just letting them play out without any direction or structure.

What is our psychic show's great objective? To abolish boredom, dissipate loneliness, generate entertainment, and spur creativity. So it is a gift full of wonderful potential—if we will make it work for us. It is our responsibility to direct this uninterrupted show, controlling the scenes, slowing down the "lines," refashioning the roles, and relaxing our minds.

But who teaches us to manage the theater of our minds? What school or university? Unfortunately, to learn this in any formal setting is rare. Education should be helping us discover the internal world—the world of the thoughts and memory and emotions—not just preparing us to live in the external world. But ultimately, healing professions exist because our schools do not focus on training us to understand what happens inside of us. So not only do we come into life without understanding its complexity; we rarely learn it in our academic institutions either. Yet understanding how we think will help us control our thoughts. That's why I want to discuss some of that thinking process next.

## Building Thoughts

One of the most complex areas of psychology is the understanding that the construction of thoughts is multi-focal and not uni-focal. According to Multi-Focal theory, this means that we don't construct thoughts solely as a conscious decision of the "self." Thoughts are created by the confluence of three additional unconscious phenomena: what are technically called the *memory trigger*, the *auto-flow phenomenon*, and the *memory window*. Knowing the entire cast of characters is almost as fundamental to mental health as eating and breathing is to the body.

To simplify these terms, think of your conscious "self" as the leading actor in the theater of the mind, and view these three phenomena as supporting actors. The greatest challenge for a person who is attempting to think correctly is to resist the attraction to leave the stage and rejoin the audience. When your mind gives in to that temptation, it essentially leaves the directing of one's thoughts to the supporting actors. But supporting actors aren't supposed to have the lead role! So developing a mind that thinks correctly involves keeping the leading actor (your conscious, decision-making "self") in the primary place onstage, while the supporting actors are fulfilling their lesser roles in the background.

## Three Supporting Actors

*1. Memory Trigger.* Also called "auto-checking of memory," this is the phenomenon that interprets and identifies each image or sound immediately, in thousandths of a second, using the "archives" of sensory information you've been storing up for your entire life. It happens spontaneously and automatically. Your mind does its own database search, so to speak, in milliseconds—checking the current stimuli from your senses (hearing, sight, taste, touch, smell) against millions of stored memories in the brain—either to recognize what you are noticing or to categorize it as new. As a result you have immediate awareness of external stimuli. Without your memory trigger, you would be miserably unable to identify sounds, images, smells, tastes, objects, or people you have encountered in the past.

Yet the memory trigger can harm us too. How? When a stimulus opens an unhealthy archive, such as a bad memory, it's the equivalent of a corrupted file. This can produce a debilitating thought that simultaneously defeats us, shuts out all the positive thoughts and ideas we have within us, and produces instant fear, insecurity, aggression, or paralysis. All of this can happen without us exercising a conscious thought. But it is precisely at this point that the person who thinks correctly must step in to direct his or her thought process so as to overcome the automatic response.

Your intelligence level has nothing to do with this series of events. People with great intellects block their minds with unhealthy memory triggers just as surely as the uneducated. One young lawyer I know of had difficulty expressing his ideas in public. Every time he opened his mouth in front of people, his memory trigger opened a window of tension in his unconscious that blocked access to the thousands of windows that contained the information he could have used to give intelligent answers. He would stutter and react as if he were a child before a beast, completely losing control of himself. Though he'd been at the top of his class in law school and had loads of knowledge stored in his brain, he didn't know how to manage his mind so that he could get the most out of it in the moment.

There are countless people in any society who, like this lawyer, don't shine in the social or professional theater because they are fragile in the psychological theater. They don't understand the workings of their mind and the traps hidden within these workings. Hopefully the information in this book will change that.

2. *Auto-flow.* This is the phenomenon that reads memory thousands of times a day and produces the great majority of thoughts in the theater of our mind. It produces the thoughts that distract us, that cheer us up, and that make us dream. Some people travel so much in the world of ideas that they are always distracted and cannot concentrate. Yet without auto-flow we would all die of boredom and loneliness.

The ideas produced by auto-flow are our greatest source of distraction and entertainment—more than TV, sports, literature, or sexual instinct. You spend most of your time involved with the world of your ideas.

The problem is that our thoughts today have become a great source of anxiety and concern—we even psychologically terrorize ourselves. If we don't learn how to direct the production of auto-flow thoughts, we will end up in a self-made prison, held captive by the anxious thoughts that modern living produces. Though we go about our lives as free people, a large number of us are internally imprisoned, stuck inside ourselves.

The correctly thinking mind drinks from the fountain of autonomy and independence, knowing that if it doesn't find freedom within itself, it won't find freedom beyond itself.

Understanding how unauthorized thoughts are constructed means assimilating one of the human mind's most complex teachings. For millennia we have believed that all thoughts are produced because we consciously wish to have them—that our thoughts are produced exclusively by the will, the "self." Besides being naive and false, this view has been a painful source of guilt.

Consider a father who imagines running over his son with his car. The man feels guilty, believing this means he wants his son dead. His mind naively assumes responsibility for ideas that it hasn't consciously produced, thoughts that it hasn't actively built, fantasies and images that it hasn't purposely created—they are simply the result of auto-flow. But without knowing the source—or how to counteract it—this loving father grows depressed, feels inferior to other dads, and punishes himself drastically, all because he doesn't understand where the thought came from. The reality is that if we don't recycle negative thoughts within five seconds, they will be filed and cannot be deleted, only reedited. We will study about this later, but understanding it is as basic as learning how to take those first steps in childhood. Unfortunately, no one teaches us how to walk within ourselves. Although teachers are irreplaceable, the educational system needs to undergo a revolution. It forms giants in science and other disciplines, but children in the understanding of ourselves. We need to be taught to know ourselves as well as we are taught other disciplines.

Without adequate knowledge about how our minds work, we can fall victim to the unconscious, just like that dad did, unable to distinguish between the thoughts we have consciously produced and the thoughts produced by the unconscious mind. In fact, we don't even realize there is a difference! And this confusion generates several psychological disorders and disturbances.

Fantasies are a prime example. They get fixed in our minds, often in childhood, and we end up blaming ourselves for them, even though we never intended to have these visions in the first place. The more we blame ourselves, the more we experience anxious reactions and anguished thoughts on the stage of our conscious mind, and the more these experiences are stored in the unconscious backstage, causing our internal conflict to grow.

3. *Memory Window* will be studied further in a subsequent chapter. For now, I will only note that it represents a region of the memory where we can anchor individual thoughts from which to build patterns of thinking. (It can also be called "memory anchor.") If the memory window is filled with positive, edifying thoughts, we can build from it fascinating ideas and concepts. If it is filled with unhealthy thoughts, the dramatic and dark ideas that surface will result only in tension and insecurity.

## When the Supporting Actors Take the Lead

Multi-Focal theory demonstrates that without these three supporting actors, the conscious "self" would not be formed. We wouldn't know who we are; we'd have no identity. Why? Because before we can become aware of ourselves, we need millions of thoughts archived in memory in the first years of life. Who produces these thoughts? The three supporting actors just mentioned: memory trigger, auto-flow, and memory window. They recognize and categorize thousands of mental images, fantasies, feelings, fears, dreams, and ideas long before we are old enough to take charge of our thoughts.

Once we are capable of taking the lead, however, the production of thoughts can become a huge villain in our quest for happiness. Trust me when I say that your greatest enemies are not outside you, but within. You can become the greatest punisher of yourself. So be careful! Thinking is an excellent, necessary, healthy, and fruitful process. But thinking *incorrectly* (too much and without care) can be a huge problem.

Let's take a look at three ways that thoughts can transform our thriving internal gardens into a cemetery of horrors.

## 1. Restless Thoughts

It's a fact that we cannot stop thinking. But when we aren't thinking consciously and willfully, the other three actors think for us. Even the most relaxed state does not completely halt the production of thoughts; it only slows them down. So our problem is not thinking—the problem is thinking excessively and anxiously. Unfortunately, too many of us have let our minds become a fountainhead of worries, where we're always occupied, even tormented, with our activities. We have barely resolved one problem before we let ten others approach the stage of our minds. Consequently, we become anxious, irritable, and sad, because a mind that is never at ease deenergizes and exhausts its owner.

You may be a specialist in solving all kinds of external problems that come your way, but if you are not able to calm your restless thoughts, you'll continually be weary. So be alert! Restless thoughts generate anxiety and stress the brain. They are powerful—able to destroy scientists, discourage the religious, and dethrone kings.

## 2. Accelerated Thoughts

It is not just the nature of thoughts that affects quality of life but their speed as well. Contrary to what we believe, though, the president of the United States does not construct thoughts any faster than the most derelict homeless person, and neither Einstein nor Freud had more psychological depth than a beggar in a third-world ghetto. Every person's brain chooses, in nanoseconds, to build an idea or thought from the billions of options circulating in the mind. In that way, every person is a genius, an artist, a scientist, a creator—worthy of equal acclaim. Yet a rapid influx of even positive thoughts can be debilitating to any of us because there is not enough time to respond to them, to implement them, or to evaluate them. That reality alone can produce anxiety and insecurity.

That's something we don't think about. We consider speed to be an asset in everything in the modern world: computers, transportation, construction, travel—the faster the better. Not so with the speed of the human mind. Information overload, the competitive drive to work harder and faster, and the paranoia of consumerism have excessively stimulated the three supporting actors in the theater of the human mind. When thoughts are built in such an accelerated fashion, people are overwhelmed. Instead of seeking to manage these thoughts, many despair and turn to various unhealthy means for blocking them out. Others pay professionals simply for the privilege of sitting down for an hour to download their overloaded minds. This is unique to our modern generation.

One of the most valuable discoveries within Multi-Focal theory is that the excessive speed of thoughts provokes ATS: *accelerated thought syndrome*. The majority of people in modern societies are afflicted with some form of ATS, although they don't know it. They may recognize the symptoms but do not know the cause.

ATS has different degrees of seriousness. In short, it is characterized by anxiety, dissatisfaction, forgetfulness, lack of concentration, restlessness, exaggerated physical tiredness (where people even wake up feeling tired), and psychosomatic symptoms (headaches, muscular pain, backaches, and the like).[1] A stressed-out person suffering from ATS can expend more energy than even ten manual laborers. But what is the value of spending that much energy if it incapacitates you over time? What's the use of being a working machine if we lose those we love, are incapable of contemplating beauty, and cannot sleep deeply at night?

When minds spend excessive amounts of energy processing sensory stimuli and then are not given adequate amounts of sleep to restore that lost energy, psychosomatic symptoms are the result. And instead of listening to our bodies, we medicate them with drugs to mask the symptoms—until physical or mental breakdown occurs.

Things like forgetfulness—failing short-term memory—are the body's cry telling us we are losing quality of life. Ironically, rather than forgetfulness being a danger sign, as many doctors believe, it is a protocol the brain uses to protect itself. It blocks certain memory archives as an attempt to slow down the rush of thoughts produced by ATS.

Often, the worst cases of ATS occur in those with the most professional responsibility—doctors, CEOs, teachers, attorneys. I once gave a series of lectures at an international medical conference on a cruise ship that circled the Greek Islands. My audience was comprised of renowned doctors, including respected medical professors. The conference organizer, a leader in medicine, was concerned about the doctors' quality of life. He had read one of my books[2] in which I criticize modern societies for becoming factories that produce stressed and anxious people who don't know how to protect their psyches and manage their thoughts, and he wanted me to speak about the workings of the mind. As part of this opportunity, I tested the audience on their psychological and psychosomatic symptoms. (This test is in appendix A.)

The result? The vast majority showed some level of accelerated thought syndrome.

Despite being aboard a beautiful ship, most of them had headaches, muscle pain, gastritis, excessive fatigue, memory deficit, irritability, emotional fluctuation, and restless minds. They were doctors, but they were ill even as they were treating ill people.

If brilliant doctors have such symptoms, how can the rest of the population be immune? If trained professionals don't know how to protect themselves, what can be expected from society in general, much less our children and teenagers who haven't even been taught that they can and must direct their thoughts?

## 3. Fixating on the Past and Future

Many people who live their lives rooted in the events of the past do so because of ATS. They have not learned to direct the thoughts that flood their minds about what has already happened. They even feel guilty or anxious about things that haven't happened yet but that *might* happen (a wayward child, a financial calamity, a disease, a career reversal, a divorce).

It's likely that more than 90 percent of our anticipatory thoughts never come true, meaning we suffer needlessly. So all the more, what we need is a way to take charge of our thoughts—a way to remain the lead actor and not allow the supporting actors to hijack the script.

## How to Manage Thoughts

DCD (Doubt—Criticize—Determine) is an excellent technique for managing thoughts and improving your mind.

1. *Doubt.* That which you believe controls you. Therefore, you must doubt everything that disturbs you. Doubting is the principle of wisdom. Dare to doubt the thoughts that say you cannot overcome your conflicts, difficulties, and challenges. Be willing to doubt the lies and negative thoughts.

2. *Criticize.* This may surprise you, but it is acceptable for you to judge that which your mind presents to you. You are not required to accept every thought that comes into your mind, and you shouldn't. You're not required to live a passive mental life either. Did you ever consider that? Indeed, you should be proactive when it comes to critiquing your thoughts, for if you don't stand against the negative and accelerated thoughts, who will? Learning to separate positive thoughts from negative thoughts is a great tool of the correctly thinking mind, and it is one you will use all the time, so it's worth developing.

3. *Determine.* Determine to be happy, secure, and strong rather than being enslaved by your conflicts. Decide to be enchanted with life, to contemplate beauty, and to fight for your dreams. On the stage of your mind, speak this to yourself and to the audience who is wondering what script you are following.

These three steps of the DCD technique must be developed in the above order. It does no good to fight for your dreams if you are not doubting and judging the negativity and guilt that flood your mind. To begin with "Determine" is to create a superficial reality, one that will not stand up under the pressures of the real world.

I recall a teenager who was desperate to gain control of her thoughts. She had started to have sexual fantasies about Jesus and believed her conscious mind was responsible for them. The result? A lovely young woman's inner tranquillity was shattered. She cried nonstop. She hated such thoughts, but the more she tried to interrupt them, the more she thought them and the more they upset her. It seemed a losing battle since she couldn't escape from herself.

When I explained to her about supporting actors, especially the auto-flow phenomenon, and showed her that she was producing unauthorized thoughts that her conscious mind really wasn't responsible for, she was fascinated and deeply relieved. She learned how to give up being the passive and frightened spectator. She taught her mind to leave the audience and begin to use the DCD technique, and as she grew, she became the manager of her thoughts and thus the director of her script. She learned to think correctly.

Like her, we all need a strategy. Even though we live in twenty-first-century America—in a time when slavery has been abolished, working conditions and wages are better than ever, human rights have been assured, and the best medical care in the world is available (not to mention the comforts and conveniences provided by technology)—and should be enjoying the greatest era of happiness and prosperity in our nation's history, we aren't. We have people trapped in addictions, more than half of our marriages end in divorce, our country has incurred massive amounts of debt, prisons are overflowing, and there is a crisis in medical care, especially among the elderly. What's wrong?

Technology has given us machines, and education has taught us how to use them for our benefit, but we still haven't learned to direct our thoughts. If people could master their thoughts, couples wouldn't divorce out of anger. People wouldn't escape into addictions as a defense against their mental torment. Peace would be pursued via creative enterprises rather than through military might.

Millions of people are suffering at this exact moment because they do not know that they can and should take the stage in the theater of their minds and read from a script that they have personally created. They don't know that they have three supporting actors that can produce either great pleasure or great pain in their lives, depending on the role they are allowed to play. Sadly, to paraphrase a prophet of old, "We are perishing for lack of understanding."

## How Our Model of Thinking Correctly Directed His Thoughts

Jesus established a new paradigm for what it means to direct one's thoughts. The kind of pressure he lived with (rejection, persecution, death threats) could have transformed him into a defensive, angry person who exited the stage of history and was never heard from again. Yet he and his mind were as calm as the surface of a placid lake. The fact that he withstood the pressures brought upon him is evidence that he was the captain of his own thoughts. So confident was he of his own inner serenity that he invited others to drink from his fountain. While that sounds egotistical in modern terms, he had the life to back it up.

Every person who is a puppet of his or her negative ideas lives like a tempestuous sea. Such people may be able to see tranquillity from afar, but they never enjoy its comfort. Every person who is controlled by negative or anticipatory thoughts lives like a fallen leaf that is carried by the wind of circumstances, without direction or stability. But not Jesus.

We don't know how, but he even knew when and how he would die. That is a faith issue, not a matter of science, so we cannot address it. But we can say from a scientific point of view that the knowledge of his impending death, and the harsh nature of it, did not diminish Jesus' cerebral energy. He was aware of tomorrow, but he didn't center today around it.

This intriguing and fascinating man stimulated his disciples to think correctly in this area. He knew how to sift through the soil of his mind and keep what was beneficial, and he guided them to do the same. Aware that "each day has enough trouble of its own,"[3] Jesus refused to speed his thoughts into the future and suffer by anticipation. Determined to live in the present, he considered future problems only long enough to acknowledge and prepare for them.

Day by day he carefully governed his thoughts and silently criticized the ideas that stole his peace. Day by day his "self" was the leading actor in the theater of his mind. And day by day, through his example, his disciples learned a strategy to improve their quality of life.

## Jesus and the School of Thinkers

Jesus also taught people how to think in general. Through his parables, his other teachings, and his example of how to handle stressful situations, he invited his disciples to become leaders of themselves, their ideas and fears, their arrogance and insecurities.

If we analyze through the eyes of psychology the texts of the four New Testament Gospels, which tell the account of his life, we find that Jesus bombarded those around him with questions. Why? Because he wanted to broaden the spectrum of their minds. He wanted to teach them to think before reacting, to question themselves, to critique their ideas, and to govern their psyche.

From my perspective, he was undoubtedly the greatest shaper of thinkers in history. His mind was so admirable that he transformed his quality of life into a garden even though his world was falling down around him and he was surrounded by downpours of discrimination. Who was this man that science cannot disprove and whose wisdom disturbs the foundations of the intellectuals?

The young Galileans who followed him, although unsophisticated, anxious, and lacking power and self-control, learned lessons that kings, politicians, and intellectuals didn't learn. He taught them to recognize their limits, to not be afraid of their failures, and to control their thoughts.

He also taught them to be sensitive and humble, to build strong relationships. He didn't want to produce warriors but people who thought and loved; people who would be capable of turning the other cheek, not as a gesture of weakness, but to surprise the careless and encourage them to think.

Walking with him was an invitation to be free and to be a leader of oneself and a director of one's thoughts. Those close to him understood that there was no use in changing the outer world without first changing one's own inner world.

---

*Thinking Correctly to Direct Your Thoughts:*
## A scientist who rose from chaos

One day a patient arrived at my office, walking slowly, closed up within his own world, his head hanging. To preserve his identity, I will call him Peter. He expressed no motivation, not even to overcome his illness. Indeed, he felt so defeated that he no longer believed any form of treatment could help him. He couldn't look me in the eye when answering my questions; he just gave me short answers. Yet here he was in my office.

Living, to him, was like carrying a heavy weight. He appeared to be unrefined and afraid of everything, especially of living. But behind this debilitated man hid an extremely cultured person, a respected physicist, and a once-brilliant college professor.

His drama was long-lived. He told me that for more than two decades he had been experiencing a series of disturbing images, among which was a bullet being shot through his son's chest. He saw his son dying in agony, and these images tormented him, controlling his mind, blocking his pleasure in living, and destroying his tranquillity—as they would for any loving father.

He had tried the two techniques that everyone uses when they have disturbing thoughts, but which rarely work: escaping from the images or forgetting them. His approach reminded me of the question I once heard a wild-animal expert pose: "If we were in Africa and suddenly a lion appeared before us in an open field, what would be the best reaction?" As the man went on to explain, forgetting that the lion exists is impossible; trying to escape would make us appetizing prey in the predator's eyes, and it would catch us and kill us in seconds. The best response, as amazing as it may seem, would be to confront the beast—try to surprise it, show it our strength. By doing so, perhaps we might have a chance of survival. The lion might retreat.

We must react in the same way against the predators of our mind. Running away from our fragility only expands it. Denying our conflicts turns us into its prey. The best way to face and surprise our beastly thoughts is to learn how to manage them and to stop being the victim of whatever imprisons us.

For more than two decades, Peter had been living in an internal prison. His mind was so inhibited, so far from thinking correctly, that it would take him more than ten minutes to open an actual door because first he had to imagine a shield to protect his son from the imaginary murderer.

The auto-flow phenomenon attached itself to Peter's memory windows, which contained the images of his son dying, and he looked at those windows continuously, obsessively reproducing the horrific images. Once registered in both his conscious and unconscious, they wouldn't leave. Thus he grew sicker and sicker, and the images multiplied. He became a puppet of his illness, and his suffering became so great that he gradually stopped working at his company.

Years later he began interrupting his classes at the university because the anguished images would appear during his classes and dominate him. Whenever this happened, Peter would stop teaching and go inside himself to begin the tiresome exercise of imagining a shield that would keep him from seeing the image of his murdered son. The more he did this, the more he produced the terrifying images. He'd go for minutes with an empty gaze, staring blankly at the perplexed students.

Peter didn't know that he had the ability to intervene against these thoughts and direct the theater of his mind. The same way that a bad business manager doesn't realize that money is being embezzled from his company until the company is bankrupt, a poor manager of thoughts does not realize he is in psychological crisis until his emotions have already given credence to the images that are destroying him.

Peter's unknowing psyche did not distinguish between the thoughts that he produced consciously and the thoughts that were produced by unconscious phenomena. Consequently, he became disturbed by what wasn't real, taking the blame for things his conscious mind wasn't guilty of. Of course, if he'd transformed those thoughts into actions, he would be responsible for them. But this is not the case with the kinds of disorders we are dealing with in this book.

In the four years before I met him, he had become so ill in his thoughts that he'd given up social contact and turned his bedroom into his world, his prison. He'd developed a deep depression in which he cried a lot. He could no longer hug or kiss his son or receive visitors. He'd seen twelve different psychiatrists, including renowned professionals, hoping to end his quiet torment. He'd taken all types of tranquilizers and antidepressants, but he didn't get better. One psychiatrist diagnosed him with psychosis, but there was no psychosis because he hadn't lost touch with reality—even in his fragile state, he knew that his mental images were not real, although he experienced them as real.

It was at this stage that I met him. During our very first sessions, I not only began to understand his story and how his traumas were formed, but I led him to understand a few things about the workings of the mind. Peter had a serious obsessive-compulsive disorder (OCD), but I told him that the time had come for him to be free, that he should learn how to be the main character of his story and stop being the victim of his conflicts.

Peter was one of the first patients I encouraged to use the technique of Doubting—Criticizing—Determining. In addition to continuing the medications he was already on, I asked him to do this exercise countless times during the week as a fundamental complement to his in-office treatment. This was as much to strengthen the leadership of his "self" as to manage his thoughts. I told him that he could do more for himself than he imagined and that his mind, like the mind of any human being, had extraordinary and powerful areas that were being underused.

He was intrigued at the possibility of leaving the audience and creating a daily production on the stage of his mind. He responded like a parched man who searches for water, like a suffocating person in search of air. He quickly learned how to wield an important psychological tool: using lucid thoughts against debilitating thoughts. Every day he described the disturbing images in notebooks and mentally doubted his control, criticized his irrationality, and demanded his inalienable right to be free.

The result was magnificent, and he conquered his OCD, which had seemed to have no solution. Those who knew him couldn't explain it, but in only six months, that forty-five-year-old man who had looked at one time as though he was a hundred, had become a new man. He began to think correctly. He became clear minded, logical, coherent, enthusiastic, secure, happy, and decisive. He improved so much that his wife went into depression because she no longer knew this man who slept in her bed! She had married an ill man who throughout the years had become increasingly inert and unresponsive. Now Peter was motivated and sociable, with a great will to work and teach. Socially he shined. Now, free of her husband's illness, his wife also needed treatment.

Peter's process of overcoming his illness wasn't magical. He needed to employ a strategy, a multi-focal plan for knowing himself, thinking correctly, and taking charge of his world. Ten years later, after seeing one of my interviews, he looked me up to tell me that he was still feeling great and that he was productive and creative.

His story is prime evidence that the human mind is capable of not only transforming a beautiful garden into arid land, but turning arid land into a garden.

## Suggested Topics for Reflection and Discussion

1. Directing thoughts involves being free to think and not being enslaved by any particular thoughts. Do your thoughts disturb you? What thoughts steal your peace?
2. Feelings of guilt steal tranquillity. Do any such feelings haunt you? Is there anything that you cannot forgive yourself for?
3. Jesus trained those closest to him to have a tranquil and serene mind. He wanted them to live amid only the actual problems of the present.

Do you suffer from anticipatory thoughts? Do things that haven't happened yet disturb you?

4. ATS is one of the most common syndromes nowadays. Do you feel that you are affected by it?

## Exercises and Reminders for Daily Practice

1. Referencing the characteristics of Principle #2—"Direct your thoughts"—that were described in the beginning of this chapter, journal about which qualities you need to develop.

2. Analyze if you have ATS syndrome using the test I gave the doctors (see appendix A). Evaluate whether you wake up feeling tired, if you are forgetful, if you have an agitated mind and lack concentration. Then write in your journal about the quality of your thoughts.

3. Be aware of the supporting actors in the theater of your mind, but don't let them dominate the stage. You and your conscious mind have to be the main actor.

4. Use the DCD (Doubt—Criticize—Determine) technique every day in the silence of your mind. Doubt everything that controls and disturbs you. Criticize each negative thought. Determine what you want to think and feel. Be the governor of your thoughts.

5. Practice not clinging to problems that haven't happened yet.

6. Try doing microrelaxation exercises throughout your day that focus your conscious mind on positive, relaxing things, such as your dreams, your life plans, and your relationships with the people you love.

## CHAPTER THREE

*Principle #3:*

# Manage Your Emotions

Most people are surprised to learn that emotions can be managed, that they don't just rise up and dictate how we must feel. The person who manages his or her emotions will

1. keep emotions under control and govern them by the use of wisdom;
2. feel feelings but not be the prisoner of them;
3. temper fears, anxiety, sadness, impulses, and aggressiveness;
4. develop tenderness, tranquillity, and tolerance;
5. expand serenity and kindness;
6. develop satisfaction and pleasure in living and in loving;
7. overcome emotions that generate psychological disorders;
8. recycle emotions that make him or her react without thinking;
9. remain young emotionally regardless of chronological age.

## True Control

Some people want to be in complete control of every aspect of their lives, inwardly and outwardly, right down to the slightest nuance and detail. Not only is this unhealthy and immature thinking, it is impossible to achieve.

Our emotions are a prime example of the futility of seeking complete control. They're in a constant state of flux, continually transforming themselves sometimes from one moment to the next: happiness can become anxiety, which can become tranquillity, which can become apprehension—all in a short period of time. Gradual fluctuations of our emotions are normal; sudden, impulsive mood swings are not. A person who explodes in anger when he was completely calm a moment before is not healthy.

While we can't stop thoughts from happening, at least they can be directed as soon as we're aware of them. Emotions are much harder to govern because they don't conform to the laws of logic (yet this is also the characteristic that makes them beautiful!). It might be logical for a mother to give up on her child after years of disappointment, but she won't. A devoted teacher will keep trying with a rebellious teenager when logic would suggest it is a waste of time. So there is a place in our lives for both rational thinking and emotion; we just need to know how to lead ourselves in both realms.

Because they are often illogical, emotions can bring enormous gain or pain, far out of proportion to what caused them in the first place. For instance, a simple, hurtful comment from the boss on a Monday morning can ruin a person's entire week. Or a card in the mail from a sweetheart can produce a week's worth of euphoria. A critical word can cause insomnia; one loss can destroy a life; a seemingly small failure can result in serious disruption to our well-being—and it's all because of our emotionality.

Yet a mind that thinks correctly trains itself to manage emotions, because this is very important to becoming a healthy person who is capable of rising above and overcoming conflict.

## Emotions, Pure but Not Simple

Emotions are the purest, most naive, most complex, and most beautiful area of the psyche. Think about it:

Without them we are rational, but with them we sometimes contradict ourselves.

Without emotions we are logical; with them we tend to distort reality.

Without emotions a strong rejection doesn't disturb us, but with emotions a despising gaze may be hard to forget.

Without emotions a great compliment doesn't excite us; with emotions a small kiss gives us chills.

Without emotions routine doesn't bother us, but with emotions it can be unbearable.

Without emotions we are predictable; with emotions we are surprising.

Without emotions we might be boring and tiresome, but with emotions we become energized and interesting.

See what I mean? Pure, complex, and beautiful—all at the same time.

Emotions also make an enormous difference in the psychological theater. They create adventure and boredom, charm and disenchantment, anxiety and tranquillity, fear and security, pleasure and depression. And to add to the drama, they cannot be managed completely! So what do we do? What approach should we take?

A correctly thinking mind understands that the goal with our emotions is to manage them as best we can by directing their significant power to achieve positive ends. The remarkable mind will also make sure the conscious "self" remains in charge rather than being ruled by emotions.

## Only One Master

Many brilliant scholars of the mind—Freud, Jung, Rogers, Skinner, Frankl, Fromm, Gardner, and others—have produced great amounts of psychological research and instruction, but they didn't have the opportunity I have had to study how memory and the leadership of the self impact our emotional energy. My theory of psychology has focused on these elements and built on previous research to shed new light on the never-ending study of the mind. Here's what I've discovered.

When dealing with emotions, there cannot be two masters. If you do not manage emotional energy—directing your emotions toward positive outcomes—your emotional energy will dominate you. Many a king and general have reigned over entire nations and ruled vast military forces but lost more important battles in the realm of their emotions, and this is where one of our primary battles occurs too.

Anger, hatred, jealousy, pride, arrogance, and fear can blindside us all—emotions are no respecter of persons. A king can be ruined by anger as easily as a commoner. Then again, responding emotionally to even positive things like praise, opportunity, and victory can lead to a downfall for anyone if we don't stay in control, because those positives can so easily become arrogance, drivenness, and greed. Not to manage emotions in these situations is to be a boat without a rudder, blown by the winds of others. The ordinary mind will be driven by his or her emotions; a correctly thinking mind will remain in the driver's seat and not give up the wheel.

Unfortunately, this subject is in many ways uncharted territory, especially in the educational realm. We teach young people how to solve problems in math and physics but not how to solve life problems, such as rejection, pain, and tragedy. Children grow up believing they should act on whatever emotions they feel: "If it feels good, do it!" But to live this way is to be managed by one's emotions—taking direction from them like a slave from a master. We do the next generation a disservice if we don't teach them what my research has shown: that emotions are not just whims—they play an important role in such practical realms as liberating creativity, rescuing the meaning of life, extinguishing fear, dissipating insecurity, and controlling aggression. Thus, we must learn about them and learn how to master them just as surely as we do any career skills.

Research in the past three decades especially has demonstrated the importance of emotional intelligence for success in life. A person who thinks correctly is not just aware of emotions but takes charge of them as much as possible so they are used for good purposes and contribute to a healthy mind and a fulfilling life.

When America's founding fathers wrote in the Declaration of Independence that mankind has the "inalienable right" to pursue "happiness," I believe they were speaking a form of "manage your emotions" language. I would put it this way: Every human being has the right to be free of unhappiness—even when others try to steal their happiness. But the only way to exercise that right is to manage one's emotions.

## Emotions Rising

Except for the emotions generated by the brain's metabolism and by psychotropic drugs such as tranquilizers and antidepressants, all of our emotions surface from the chains of conscious and unconscious thoughts that are produced when the memory is read. They are the fruit of that process.

To break it down into less technical terms, every time you have a feeling, you first produce a thought, even if you aren't aware of the thought behind it. This happens throughout the day, but also while you sleep. That's exactly why you can go to bed happy but wake up in a bad mood. It's because your subconscious mind—which we've already said never sleeps—read your memory while you were sleeping and produced chains of disturbing thoughts. These became unsettling dreams that aroused emotion and subsequently generated a foul mood. And voilà! You woke up on the wrong side of the bed through no conscious effort of your own!

The process of constructing emotions is so quick that we aren't aware of it and can't stop it. Emotions are like thoughts in that way. Fortunately, our goal here is not to stop the emotions but to do a better job of managing them. In the previous chapter we saw how the memory trigger opens a group of archives, which I call the memory window, when it receives a stimulus. This window is read by your memory just as you read a window that opens on your computer (only much quicker), and that internal reading immediately produces thoughts that create emotions. Left to themselves, they quickly career out of control and wreak havoc in our lives. But if our conscious selves take hold of the wheel, those emotions and thoughts add up to rich experiences.

Let me give you an example. When you watch a horror movie, your rational self knows that it is pretend; that there are a large number of people standing just behind the camera, who are creating a fictional scenario—cameramen, the director, lighting and special-effects people. Yet when the slowly opening door creaks on its rusty hinges, the memory trigger automatically throws open a window that contains your fears—real or imagined—from the past. This produces unconscious thoughts that create emotional energy. All of this happens in fractions of a second.

Though you promised yourself you wouldn't be afraid, fear appeared in the theater of your mind before you could influence it. So your greatest challenge then becomes taking control of and managing your fear after it appears.

In any given situation, the first thoughts and emotions arise before we're even aware of them. We must then leave the audience of the mind, go onstage, and direct the play that they're enacting so that our conscious self stays in the lead.

This is truly where our wars and acts of violence against each other originate, as well as our lesser daily conflicts. Hundreds of "theatrical" moments take place every day on the stage of our minds without our conscious consent, and too often we just let them play out. A father's correction of his teenage son escalates into an hour-long, full-blown argument where the same topic gets rehashed over and over. People suffer an injustice at work and keep anguishing over it until they are sick to their stomachs. Timid people who have a social commitment to fulfill suffer for weeks beforehand, unable to sleep. These good people sit back and watch the horror movie in their minds, "going with the flow," unaware that they can improvise and turn the plot onstage in their favor; unaware that they don't have to experience such emotions.

That is why it is so important that we be trained—in school and at home—to manage our emotions, our thoughts, our selves. The more we're taught how to do this growing up, the less we will have to depend on psychiatry and psychology as adults. Education—formal and informal, for both the inward and outward life—is truly the foundation for quality of life.

# A Strategy for Taking Charge

To manage emotions we must practice the DCD (Doubt—Criticize—Determine) technique, just as we did for directing thoughts—only in this case we will doubt the unhealthy content of our emotions and question the reasons for our reactions, criticize our anxiety, and demand to be free in that moment. In addition, when tempted to react emotionally in unhealthy ways, choosing silence first is yet another means of arousing our inner leader to action.

If we don't consciously doubt and criticize the unhealthy emotional scripts that are rehearsing in our minds, we will always be the victims of psychological miseries and emotional disorders. Following are some of the most common ones:

## Anxiety and Psychosomatic Symptoms

There is a type of "anxiety" or tension that is healthy—that encourages us to break with conformity, fight for our dreams, and nourish our curiosity. There's another type that is chronic, intense, obstructive, and destructive. The kind we will experience is determined by our skill at managing our emotions.

Anxiety is a psychic state in which an excessive number of thoughts are produced, resulting in tense emotions. The basic symptoms are ones we've probably all experienced in some fashion: irritability, intolerance, emotional instability, restlessness, sleep disorders, and sometimes psychosomatic symptoms such as headaches, gastritis, dizziness, a lump in the throat, arterial hypertension, hair loss, or muscular pain. The psychosomatic symptoms appear when anxiety isn't resolved.

We now know that psychological disorders can trigger a series of physical illnesses, from heart attacks to certain types of cancer. The anxiety is transmitted to the brain's cortex and discharged in some area of the body, usually an organ. Because of its impact, we call this "organ shock." In the heart it produces tachycardia (rapid heart rate); in the skin, prurigo (itching); in the lungs, breathlessness. Some people develop these symptoms more easily than others.

There are several types of anxiety:

- phobias (exaggerated fear when facing a phobic object or situation);
- panic syndrome (the sudden sensation that one will die or pass out);
- OCD—obsessive-compulsive disorder (fixed ideas accompanied sometimes by ritualistic or repetitive behavior);
- GAD—generalized anxiety disorder (restlessness and irritability frequently accompanied by psychosomatic symptoms);
- PTSD—posttraumatic stress disorder (anxiety following physical and psychological traumas such as personal loss, job loss, divorce, accidents, and war).

Don't despair if you experience one or more of these things. All of them can be overcome, for nothing is irreversible when it comes to the human psyche. All it takes is learning the skill of emotion management.

## Depression

There are various types of depression, for instance,

- major depression (someone who has always been happy but for some reason—loss, frustration, separation, or negative thoughts—has a depressive crisis);
- dysthymic depression (someone whose typical emotional state is to be sad or pessimistic, usually since adolescence); and
- bipolar depression (someone with alternating moods that include fluctuating periods of humor, excitation, and depression).

In some cases of depression there are serotonin deficits, and sometimes there are genetic influences, but there is no such thing as "genetic condemnation"—"Well, your parents suffered from it, so you're bound to also." Even if the parents within a family are depressive, their children can be happy, sociable, creative, and enterprising if they learn how to think correctly and manage their thoughts, protect their emotions, contemplate beauty, and work out their frustrations and disappointments.

Many depressed patients are wonderful people who simply don't know how to protect themselves emotionally through self-awareness and boundaries with others. As a result, they overly suffer the pain of others; they give too much of themselves; they are hypersensitive to the point where an offense from the past can echo within them interminably. But the most serious depressive symptoms are despondency, loss of pleasure, diminishing libido, sleep and appetite disorders, suicidal ideas, excessive fatigue, and social isolation.

Depression is not a temporary state of sadness that lasts a few hours or days. It is a disease that represents the last stage of human suffering; therefore it is important for depression to be treated by a medical professional, preferably an experienced psychiatrist. Treatment with anti-depressants can and should be complemented with psychotherapy.

## Suicide Risk

Sadly, each year around the world, one million people commit suicide. More people die from suicide than from murder.

But it is important to understand that when people contemplate or attempt suicide, they are not trying to kill themselves—they are trying to kill their emotional pain, anguish, and desperation. Philosophically speaking, every thought about death is a manifestation of life: those who think of dying are, deep down, hungry and thirsty for life. They are desperately trying to destroy the anguish they feel, to escape it, even if death is the result.

Many of my depressed patients who have contemplated suicide experienced an improved quality of life when they discovered that they really didn't wish to die but to live—they simply wanted to live free of their misery. Once they left the audience of their emotions and learned how to rescue their inner leader, they were no longer victims.

If you have relatives or friends who are depressed and have lost the courage to live, listen to them without criticizing them. Don't give them superficial advice either; lend them your heart. Tell them that they are strong, that they have a hunger and thirst for living. Encourage them to seek treatment without guilt, for we should never give up on life. We can face our losses and disappointments with boldness—our correctly thinking mind makes this possible. We can criticize, confront, and control our unhealthy emotions every day, if only we will learn how.

## Leading with Healthy Emotions

Keep this in mind as you read the rest of this chapter: *unhealthy emotions love passive people, but healthy emotions love people who lead them.*

If you practice governing your emotions, you'll notice a big difference after only a few months. Your life will be more tranquil, you'll feel freer, and you'll be able to dream—to set goals for yourself and go after them. You will become more and more enchanted with your own existence, and sensitivity and serenity will gradually become part of your personality. You will leave conformity and passivity behind and discover the previously misused and misunderstood capacity and vigor of a mind that thinks correctly.

## How Our Model of Thinking Correctly Managed His Emotions

It was the last day of a great Jewish festival in Jerusalem, and a group of temple guards were looking for Jesus of Nazareth. In their minds, he had to be arrested and silenced right away because his preaching was undermining the religious stability of the Jews, and therefore of Palestine—which was under Roman control. He was gaining a large following; therefore the movement surrounding him was considered subversive and divisive by both the Jewish and Roman authorities. Jerusalem itself was like a powder keg, given the influx of tens of thousands of visitors for the festival, and Jesus was considered a threat to national security.

Did Jesus manifest fear in the face of this turmoil? No. He stood up in the midst of the crowd at the high point of the festival and spoke words that shook not only those who heard them but those who have read them ever since: He encouraged all those who thirst for quality of life to come to him and drink. He declared to thousands of people that whoever learned his secrets would have an inextinguishable source of happiness and tranquillity within themselves.[1]

Who was this man to preach about the pleasure of living while he was surrounded by terror? Who was this man who spoke of life when he was staring death in the face? He was the most accomplished quality-of-life specialist, the most accomplished thinker, the world has ever known. None of the rest of history's most brilliant minds—Plato, Aristotle, Bacon, Descartes, Kant, Hegel—have ever considered making a speech like that (possibly because there isn't a single philosopher or psychiatrist who doesn't pass through the valleys of anxiety, disappointment, and sad moods). Many psychiatrists especially, because they constantly work with the miseries of the psyche, lose their own enchantment with life; they lose their joy and passion, competently taking care of others but forgetting to tend to their own emotions.

Only someone as internally healthy as Jesus was capable of such a bold invitation! Only someone who could manage his emotions and not focus on criticism or stress was capable of passing so peacefully through life. This man from Nazareth refused to be enslaved by fear, despair, negative thoughts, or any external circumstances. He insisted on being free within himself.

The apostle John tells us that the temple guards returned to the high priest without Jesus. When questioned as to why they had not brought him in—why a group of armed men had failed to arrest a single unarmed man—they said, "No one ever spoke the way this man does."[2] They were amazed by his attitude. They saw a serene person in a land of hatred, a great leader who led his own emotions first.

Jesus preached about joy in a place where there was no reason at all to be happy. He talked about the meaning of life when others were trying to end his life. He created his own reasons to be happy and was free to feel exactly how he wanted to feel.

Many people have reasons to be happy, but they are sad and anxious. They aren't deprived socially—they have a good family, friends, and adequate finances. But they are specialists in the complaint department. Instead of governing their emotions, they are governed *by* them. Dissatisfied emotions demand a lot and give little. Healthy emotions, like Jesus experienced, make a lot from almost nothing.

## Facing the Chaos of Emotions

There is no question that Jesus, our model of thinking correctly, went through emotional chaos in his life. On the night he was eventually arrested, he was in a garden with three of his disciples when a crowd sent by the Jewish high priest came for him, led by one from his own inner circle ( Judas Iscariot). Jesus was in that garden praying, preparing himself for what he had said all along was coming. (There would be four trials between the Jews and the Romans, followed by his crucifixion.)

In order to bear witness to what he had taught for three years, he would have to bear his suffering differently than any other man had ever done: exercise love instead of hate and forgiveness instead of condemnation, and die in peace rather than in emotional turmoil. And he succeeded in doing just that—so much so that one of the Roman guards even declared that he had to be who he'd said he was because he responded so differently than any other person.[3]

From a psychological standpoint, how did Jesus prepare himself for such an experience? He began readying himself emotionally ahead of time. He reviewed all the painful possibilities he faced—and it was not easy. Indeed, in the garden he told his disciples, "My soul is overwhelmed with sorrow to the point of death."[4] Today someone in a similar circumstance might say, "I'm scared to death!" He even exhibited a very rare symptom, seen only in times of excruciating stress: *hematidrose*, or bloody sweat.[5] But, at the height of the tension, he took to the stage of his mind and began to direct himself, which resulted in him managing his emotional response to the situation. Based on his life project as he understood it, he cried out to God, saying he was willing to do whatever it took to accomplish the objective. He chose to submit his own immediate well-being to the greater goal of his father.

Who was this man who made poetry amid chaos? Who was this man who ignored the scream of billions of cells in his body that were imploring him to run away or, at the very least, to defend himself? Only a person with an amazing and radiant mind, a mind that could think of others while it was suffering. Jesus' love for humanity leaves psychology and philosophy in astonishment. It is his boldness in rescuing his inner leader at a moment when it could have been hijacked by fear and anxiety that makes him stand out.

He remained in control of not only his intellect but his emotions. Even though realistic images of horror had entered the theater of his mind, instead of becoming passive and giving in to despair, Jesus became active—the lead writer in the script of his life and the director of the theater of his mind. He decided not to become enslaved by his emotions or become a prisoner of his thoughts or his circumstances.

He intuitively went through the DCD exercise in his own way: He *doubted* the strength of fear; he *criticized* the disturbing ideas that came to his mind; he *determined* to remain free and in control. Internally, he left the audience of his mind, went onstage, and ultimately took charge of that complex territory.

---

*Think Correctly to Manage Your Emotions:*

## A doctor is freed from panic

Antony was a skilled surgeon, secure and swift with a scalpel. He was also a sensitive and sociable person. Yet one day, while nearing the end of a routine surgery, his heart began to palpitate, and he began to get cold sweats. Growing short of breath and thinking he was going to pass out, he asked an assistant to finish for him.

Upon finding a place to lean, he soon recovered from the crisis and attributed this incident to stress and exhaustion caused by overwork. Even though he had felt an intense fear at that moment in the operating room, he assured himself it was nothing to be alarmed about. A few days later, however, Antony had a repeat episode with the same symptoms.

It was at that point that a fear of dying came over him, accompanied by despair. He dealt with life and death almost every day—other people's. Now, though, the issues had become intensely personal. It was his turn to wrestle with the end of existence. He became disturbed with questions he had rarely asked: "What is death? What is the last instant of life like? Is there an afterlife in which I could see my children again?"

When these episodes would strike, countless thoughts would steal his peace, and in a matter of seconds his mind would turn into a stage of fear. He'd be convinced that he was going to die at any moment.

Antony didn't know it, but he was having panic attacks. Though his health was excellent, his mind was fixed on thoughts about the end of life, and his emotions lived out the fantasy of death in those moments as if it were real. The emotional charge was so great that he had a series of psychosomatic reactions in an attempt to escape from his "enemies." But there were no real enemies. They were all in his head.

The attacks occurred even at his office. He talked to an assortment of colleagues, including cardiologists. He underwent several tests— electrocardiograms, echocardiograms, etc.—and never found anything that justified his symptoms. He consulted with a few psychiatrists who diagnosed him with panic syndrome, but medication did not defeat his problem. With the failure of treatment, he lost his confidence to perform surgery and, after a few years, quit clinical work altogether.

This humane and intelligent man had become imprisoned by fear that not only caused him to abandon medicine but to isolate himself from others. He was like so many who suffer panic attacks: one of the basic characteristics is social phobia. The patient becomes afraid of being in public—of going to parties, stores, and restaurants—for fear he will embarrass himself or have another episode with no one around to help. Though there are millions of people around the world who are victims of this totally treatable syndrome, Antony felt like an emotional invalid.

Antony came to see me, but ironically he wouldn't look me in the eye. His speech was shaky, and he was very suspicious of everyone and everything. His self-esteem had bottomed out, and he was as unhappy as he could be. However, gradually, my treatment stimulated him to gain freedom from his emotional bondage.

I guided him to understand the process of personality formation—how the first panic attacks registered "privileged status" in his memory, constructing a "killer" or destructive window that was closing out the positive thoughts and producing new, negative attacks. I told him that this mechanism is universal and is present in many psychological conflicts; he wasn't the only person to experience it. I also showed him that the big problem is not what opens the window—the frustration, offense, accident, or panic attack itself—but the privileged status we give it in our unconscious and upon every subsequent reading of that window in our memory. In essence, it sets off an internal alarm each time, telling us we're in trauma. This reading produces further traumatic experiences that are again registered in the memory, which then expands the killer window and activates the cycle of disease, all while imprisoning the mind and blocking creativity, security, tranquillity, motivation, and even intellectual capacity.

I showed Antony that, contrary to what some psychiatric professionals think, it is impossible to delete or erase the memory. Memory can only be rewritten. I used medication as a supporting actor in his treatment but told him that he was the main actor. Antony needed to arouse the leader of his inner self against his negative thoughts and give his emotions a blast of reality. I encouraged him to doubt the dictatorship of fear, to criticize his passive and timid posture in the face of tension points generated by the panic attacks, and to determine to be free. This way he would be the author of his own story and reedit his unconscious film, therefore taking action in areas where medication had no access.

Antony did this day by day. He put his emotions under the control of his conscious mind. He learned to continually monitor and manage what was going on within him. And the result? He developed tranquillity and serenity in his everyday life. He freed his emotions from bondage. He relit the flames of security and expanded the roots of his self-esteem. And after fifteen years away from his beloved profession, he once again returned to medicine and was the competent, social person his friends had known him to be. Only now he was even better, for he understood—because he'd witnessed it for himself—that the mind is naturally extraordinary, though its secrets are often hidden from us and its powerful tools underused.

His family was impressed with the way he overcame his emotional chaos and became a loving, secure person again. In fact, his eighteen-year-old daughter told me, with emotion in her voice and tears in her eyes, that she had grown up without a father. Now they have long and pleasant conversations together. After fifteen years, father and daughter have found each other. They had been so close yet so far away.

Antony's patients enjoy being attended by him more than other doctors. They see in him a humane, attentive physician who is not only interested in prescribing medication and performing surgery but in relieving their anxieties and fears. After crossing a lonely desert, Antony has trained his mind to think correctly and become a true manager of his emotions.

## Suggested Topics for Reflection and Discussion

1. Governing emotions means being free to feel, but not being shackled by feelings. It means equipping yourself to dissipate fear, recycle anxiety, and overcome insecurity. What kind of emotion disturbs you? Are you a patient person or an impulsive person?

2. Emotions are triggered by thoughts. Do you take action when you

notice that irritation, aggression, and fear have been triggered, or do you simply stand back and watch them play out?

3. Jesus wasn't a slave of circumstances; he was capable of inviting people to drink from his internal well no matter the situation. Do you invite those you love to draw from the well of your tranquillity and joy? Do you suffer over little things? How do you protect your emotions?

4. There are several types of anxiety and depression listed in this chapter. Do you have any of these disorders? Do you have the courage to open your emotional heart to those close to you, or do you hide your pain? Do you know how to ask for help?

## Exercises and Reminders for Daily Practice

1. Referencing the characteristics of Principle #3—"Manage your emotions"—described in the beginning of this chapter, journal about which qualities you need to develop.

2. Evaluate and journal about your emotional quality of life. Analyze if you require too much to be happy, if you expect too much in return from others, if you are too worried about what others think of you, if small offenses hurt you beyond what they should.

3. Record whether you've been stressed and have manifested psychosomatic symptoms.

4. Don't run away from your emotional pain; confront your emotions and rethink them. If you flee from suffering, emotions will become a monster for you because you will have given them the power. If you face your emotions, they can be overcome, recycled, and domesticated like a pet.

5. Remember, *when we are abandoned by the world, the loneliness is bearable; when we abandon ourselves, the loneliness is almost incurable.* So do not give up on yourself! You are worth investing in!

6. Don't turn your emotions into a garbage can for your problems. Protect yourself by using the DCD technique.

7. Think before reacting in the face of offenses.

8.  Manage your emotions to have hope, to toast life, and to contemplate beauty.

Don't forget that while the process of learning to think correctly can give you the bricks, only you can build with them. Correct thinking can show you to the helm, but only you can navigate the waters of emotion.

## CHAPTER FOUR

*Principle #4:*

# Protect Your Memory

All of us have memory and memories, but few of us understand how memory works. The more we know about memory, the more we will be able to use it as a tool to develop a higher quality of life and achieve the happiness we seek. Here are eight summary statements about the power of memory:

1. Memory is the archive of the secrets of human personality. Our task is to access and benefit from the information in that archive.
2. Memory can be an aid in expanding the art of thinking.
3. Memory is the soil in which ideas and emotions take root and flourish.
4. Emotions play a role in opening up the territory of memory and constructing chains of thoughts.
5. There are trauma and conflict zones in our memory that we must understand.
6. Memory can become cluttered with psychological and social "garbage."
7. The unconscious "movie" of memory can be reedited with the proper tools.

> 8. Memory can be protected and stressful stimuli filtered out with the proper techniques.

## The Involuntary Nature of Memory

A teacher was severely offended by a student's rude and inhumane behavior. He tried to forget about the student so as not to be tormented by the memory of his actions. But the more he tried to forget about the student, the more he thought about him. Whenever he saw the student, his feelings about him returned.

Why couldn't the teacher forget about the student? Because the "keeper" of your memory, the memory register, is automatic and does not depend on human will. As much as you might like to, you don't sign in when you want to remember something and then sign out when you want to forget. Your experiences, thoughts, and emotions get logged in. Period.

Unlike your computer, you don't control the content of your memory; it is involuntary—subject to the automatic memory registry (AMR) phenomenon. Where thinking correctly comes in is in learning how to "protect" what gets registered in your conscious memory. Those who take care in this area will expand central characteristics of their mind. They'll be more imaginative, insightful, and illuminated, as well as more capable of working through mistakes and frustration.

## The Further Truth About Memory

We humans have always given memory credit for functions it doesn't have. We've claimed it's dependent on our wills; we've believed we could erase our memories and live as if things never happened or entered our consciousness in the first place. But these things are not true. In order to expand our minds and improve our quality of life, we must understand the role of memory and the tools we have for working with it, for every day—as you're about to see—we are planting either flowers or weeds in the soil of our memory. Unfortunately, because we don't understand how our memory works, we don't till the most complex soil of our personalities, and therefore we fail in the agriculture of our minds. But with this chapter, we can start to change that.

Every idea, thought, reaction, moment of emotion, and experience is imprinted in your memory and becomes part of the patchwork quilt of your story—the movie of your life. The more we try to forget those experiences of hurt, loss, or rejection, the more deeply they get registered within us and the more they will be accessed, or "read," by our unconscious mind. The more those negative memories get read, the more they will lead to the construction of thousands of additional thoughts about exactly the incident we don't want to remember!

The best way to filter stressful experiences is not by being angry, feeling hatred, or rejecting or complaining about them (indeed, these reactions make them worse!) but to

- understand them;
- criticize them;
- see them multi-focally, that is, from different angles;
- use them as an opportunity to grow;
- determine not to be enslaved by them.

## The Effect of Emotions

The greater the "emotional volume" of an experience, so to speak, the more the registry has to work with, and thus the greater chance of its memory being "read." Think about your life: your ever-active senses register millions of experiences—and therefore millions of memories—a year. But it is the experiences with the greatest emotional content that keep being recalled, right?—such as the ones involving loss, joy, praise, fear, or frustration.

Where are the experiences registered? Initially in the CUM (continuous usage memory), which is the memory used in everyday activities—the conscious memory. Intense experiences are registered in the conscious center and from then on will be read continuously. Over time, as the memories lose their intensity, they are less frequently recalled and begin to dislocate to the peripheral part of memory called EM (existential memory).

Here's an example. When someone compliments you, you register it in the CUM. You "read" this compliment several times on the day it happens. The following day, you don't read it as much. The following week, you may barely read it at all, and within a month, it seems to have vanished. However, this compliment hasn't been erased; it has simply gone to the unconscious territory, to the EM. It will continue influencing your personality, but with less intensity.

Another example shows the detrimental side of this phenomenon: Let's say you have just finished giving a lecture during which you lost your train of thought. You were unable to say what you wanted to; you were nervous; people noticed your insecurity. You registered this experience in the CUM. If your mind is thinking correctly, it will filter this experience through critical thinking and understanding. The event will thus be registered without great intensity and isn't likely to affect you much the next time you teach. If you failed to protect your memory, this incident will very likely be registered with a great deal of intensity. The application of this Think Correctly principle determines the difference between a misused mind and one that is healthy and mature.

In the latter case, the negative experience will be read frequently in the days ahead, and in similar scenarios, and will produce thousands of prohibitive thoughts that will be registered and thereby create a conflict, or trauma, zone. Thus, the incident will not go to the EM. It will stay in the CUM as an unhealthy window. Our goal is to create as few of these conflict zones as possible.

Our emotions not only determine the quality of our experiential registry but also the degree to which the memory is opened. Tense emotions can close that window where memory is read, making us react by instinct instead of with rationale. This important subject is also the theme of another principle of thinking correctly: learning the art of self-dialogue, yet to be discussed. In it we will be studying in-depth the killer windows that destroy the capacity to think properly.

If you've ever noticed that you are sometimes incoherent when facing small problems and lucid when facing big ones, well, now you know: it's your memory at work. Our ability to cope is not affected by the size of our external problems but by the opening or closing of the areas where memory is read. Small problems such as a scornful look from a loved one or the sight of a snake can generate an anxiety crisis that closes positive areas of memory and obstructs rational thinking. In some cases, the volume of anxiety or suffering can be so intense that you react without any sense at all. Nonetheless, in certain instances, we open beautiful windows and produce thoughts that cultivate beautiful emotions. In others, we open unhealthy windows that promote problems, not only for us but for others.

I once saw a father and his teenage son get into a physical fight right in front of me because of a foolish problem. The surface reason was small, but it triggered the monstrous images that one had of the other and generated a serious crisis between them. Such things happen all the time. A poorly handled criticism can break up a friendship. Being discriminated against can keep you locked up internally for life. Being disappointed by a loved one can generate intense insecurity. A public mistake can block your intellect. Being labeled with a cruel nickname can shut down the mind and generate serious conflict. That is why you want to not only be careful about your words and actions toward others, but protect your memory as well.

Don't ever forget to be the director of your psyche; to rewrite your thoughts, administer your emotions, doubt your incapacity, question your fragility, and see things from different angles. Without protecting yourself, you will miss out on the extraordinary quality of life that you desire, and the horizons of your mind will not expand like they could.

# Never Deleted

With computers it is an easy task to delete or erase information. Not so with humans. In fact, it is impossible to erase a person's memory except in cases where a person suffers from brain lesions such as tumors, cranial-encephalic trauma, or cellular degeneration. You can try with all your might to erase, erase, erase. You can focus all your energy on destroying the memory of those who have hurt you as well as eliminating the most difficult moments of your life, but you will not be successful, even with a mind that is thinking correctly.

So what can you do to help yourself? In addition to the steps we've already discussed, you must act every time you have an experience that generates a charge of anxious emotion. So there are two ways of solving conflicts, traumas, and psychological disorders:

1. Reedit the unconscious movie.
2. Build windows parallel to the unhealthy windows in memory.

The second solution, building parallel windows, will be covered in another chapter. Here we'll learn how to reedit the unconscious movie. Reediting memory archives means registering new experiences over the negative experience.

When we apply the DCD technique (Doubt—Criticize—Determine) in a moment of tension, we produce new experiences that are registered where the unhealthy experiences were stored. Consider a man who, for no apparent reason, is consistently aggressive and critical toward those around him. If he applies the DCD technique daily to his negative behavior—*doubting* the legitimacy of it; *criticizing* its value; *determining* to replace it with more appropriate behavior—he can reedit the movie of his behavior in his unconscious within three months.

He will become noticeably different—kinder and more positive. He may still have negative impulses, but they will be fewer and less intense. One of the most important roles of the "self" is acting as the author of its own story—rewriting the effects of its past and reediting its unconscious movie. Changing, reorganizing, or transforming the human mind is not easy, but it is possible. It depends on training, perseverance, objectivity, and reeducation.

## To Care for Memory Is to Care for Your Life

An ordinary mind busies itself with what is going into its "computer," but a mind that thinks correctly goes beyond to also give attention to the miseries being archived in its memory. As we've learned, being unable to recall a negative experience doesn't mean it has gone away; it's simply been displaced from conscious memory (CUM) to unconscious memory (EM). It's still part of us. Consequently, we create unhealthy neighborhoods in the big city of memory, contaminating its air, filling its streets with potholes, and cutting off its lights.

Don't forget this metaphor. We can gradually lose our emotional health if we don't filter the stressful stimuli, reedit the unconscious movie, and protect our memory.

It is possible to have an unhappy adult life despite having had a happy childhood. But it is also possible, through the management of thoughts and emotions, to have a healthy adult life despite a traumatic childhood There are rich people who live miserably and there are paupers who make each day a new day. The latter don't have designer clothes, luxurious cars, or houses on the beach, but their memories are gardens where rich emotions and beautiful thoughts spontaneously bloom. Their winters are short and their springs are long.

If you wish to work through the functions of memory with wisdom, you need to live the other Think Correctly principles explained in this book. By now you likely understand that one principle depends on the other. Decide to change your lifestyle if it is stressful; spend time contemplating the beautiful, simple things in life; free your creativity; practice controlling your thoughts; and give your emotions a reality check. If you do this, your days will be happy and the quality of your life high. Though you may have deserts to cross, you will remain refreshed.

## How Our Model of Thinking Correctly Managed His Memory

Jesus reached spectacular levels of kindness and calmness. He never berated prostitutes, tax collectors, elders, or the young about their flaws and failures. Neither did he give up on them. Offenses, criticism, aggressiveness, betrayal—even denial and rejection—weren't deposited as garbage in his memory, because he knew his peace was worth gold.

Let's analyze one of the best-known demonstrations of rejection in history—the betrayal of Jesus by his friend Judas Iscariot—and see how Jesus protected his memory, filtered stressful stimuli, and helped his disciples develop the art of memory management.

The Master of masters, throughout his journey, received small amounts of money from friends for his and his disciples' sustenance. To whom did Jesus entrust these funds? To Judas. Was he being naive when he gave Judas such a responsibility? Not at all. He was aware of his disciple's fragile character, but he never gave up on him. Why? Because he wasn't afraid of being robbed by Judas; he was concerned about losing him.

Jesus' attitude reveals that he had clear goals for his disciples. Molding their compassion, their art of thinking, and their love for one another was more important than all the money in the world. He wanted Judas to review his story while he handled the group's finances. Judas may have been the most cultured of the disciples, but he was the least prepared for life.

Jesus' willingness not to reveal Judas's faulty character was an indication of how he protected his memory. Jesus didn't contaminate his memory by mulling over negative thoughts regarding his disciple. He knew that those who are dishonest steal from themselves. What do they steal? They steal their own tranquillity, their serenity, and their love for life. He wanted Judas to learn how to think before reacting and to value what he, the Master, loved the most.

Judas's biggest mistake wasn't the betrayal of Jesus but his failure to learn transparency and realize that his greatest problems were within him. He accumulated rubble in his memory, especially during the last months before he betrayed Jesus, and it limited him.

In the beginning, he was fascinated with Jesus' power and eloquence. But little by little Judas became frustrated with Jesus because he didn't do what Judas hoped he would: take the political throne of Israel. Judas didn't understand that Jesus wanted the throne of the human heart, which can only be won over with freedom, wisdom, and love.

## Fascinating the Intellectuals

Jesus' attitudes fascinate intellectuals. During the Last Supper—his "going away" meal with his disciples—Jesus announced his death and said, with a broken heart, that one of the disciples would betray him. Shaken, they all wanted to know the name of the betrayer. But Jesus never exposed people's mistakes publicly.

The best way to block someone's growth is to embarrass him or her in public. Jesus wouldn't tell the disciples the betrayer's name. They insisted. So, demonstrating an admirable humanity, instead of accusing Judas, Jesus gave him a piece of bread.[1] His betrayer wanted to harm him, but the model of thinking correctly wanted to satiate him. He knew that Judas was starving for personal peace.

No one but Judas realized the meaning when Jesus handed him the bread. Once again, Jesus demonstrated a strength and serenity as bright as the sun. He told Judas without fear: "What you are about to do, do quickly."[2] He didn't criticize, pressure, or control him. He had the boldness to tell Judas that if he wished to betray him, he could do so anytime he wanted. Never in the annals of history has anyone had such an altruistic attitude toward his betrayer. Once again I affirm: Jesus wasn't afraid of being betrayed by Judas; he was concerned about losing him.

By giving him a piece of bread instead of attacking him publicly, and by encouraging him to freely do what he wanted, Jesus was sweetly calling for Judas to rethink his story, protect his memory, and become the leader of himself.

Others in history would've done well to follow Jesus' lead. But too many have chosen Judas's route instead. Joseph Stalin, for instance. He was a big man on the outside—leader of the Soviet Communist Party in Russia—but so small on the inside that he killed millions of people. Among his victims were dozens of his own friends. Why? Because he was paranoid. The mere fact that he suspected his friends were betraying him was reason enough to condemn them and publicly declare them traitors. As one of history's foremost executioners—an insensitive man incapable of feeling others' pain—he dominated the mind and fate of people, all because of his fear of betrayal and losing power.

Jesus was different. Even knowing that he would be betrayed by Judas and later denied by Peter,[3] he directed his thoughts, managed his emotions, protected his memory, and gave these two men complete freedom to do as they chose.

During the act of betrayal, Jesus gave another proof that he wanted to win Judas over. Judas arrived with an escort of soldiers, even though he knew that Jesus was profoundly docile. All that would be needed to identify him to the soldiers was a kiss on the cheek. So he walked in front of them and kissed the one who had been his friend.

Would you allow your betrayer to greet you this way? Lots of people have never spoken again to a friend after a disappointment. Jesus allowed himself to be kissed! At this, Jesus gazed at Judas and said, "Friend, do what you came for. . . . are you betraying the Son of Man with a kiss?"[4]

A betrayer treated with such kindness is unheard-of in history. Love has never reached such heights. Jesus called the traitor "friend"—and he didn't lie. As the most faithful and conscientious of men, he kept his word to the end. He had said in the Sermon on the Mount that we should turn our other cheek to our enemies and love them.[5] He loved Judas and turned the other cheek to him at the greatest moment of psychological tension. He wanted to win Judas over and keep him from committing suicide.

Only someone with an exceptionally healthy mind is capable of such an attitude and action. No psychiatrist has ever come close to having this level of maturity. Freud banished from his psychoanalytical family those who disagreed with his ideas, as did his friends Jung and Adler. Jesus acknowledged his betrayer as a friend and made an effort to teach him how to protect his emotions and his memory.

## How We Betray Our Ability to Make Good Things Happen

Those who analyze these facts through the eyes of psychology and psychiatry have to bow before Jesus' greatness. Less than an hour before, as he sweat drops of blood in the Garden of Gethsemane in agony over his immediate future, Jesus was experiencing extreme stress. Yet with Judas he was functioning at the height of his intellect. No one has ever loved so much, included so many, invested so much, and given so many chances to people who deserved so little. Unfortunately, Judas didn't understand his teacher's language.

Through the automatic memory register phenomenon, Judas's betrayal went deeply into the soil of his own memory. Jesus was able to keep it from registering too intensely, but Judas left the Last Supper feeling disturbed. He realized Jesus' incomprehensible amicability but did not allow himself to be reached by it. What is worse, he began to gravitate around the conflict zone (killer window) that he had created.

The auto-flow phenomenon began to rapidly read this conflict zone and produced thousands of thoughts without the authorization of Judas's conscious "self." These thoughts, in turn, began to feed Judas's feelings of guilt and tormented him intensely. Hence, the auto-flow phenomenon, which can generate pleasure, generated a horror scene instead. Judas wasn't the author of his story but the victim of his mistakes. Unfortunately, in spite of Jesus' efforts, he gave up on himself.

Peter's mistake wasn't less serious than Judas's, but he allowed himself to be reached by his teacher. His mistakes cut into the coarse stone of his mind and produced a diamond. He learned from Jesus how to be understanding and kind toward all people. He learned that a human being's wisdom isn't in the absence of mistakes but in using one's mistakes as a foundation of growth.

Over the years of practicing psychiatry and researching the secrets of the human mind, I have discovered that we don't know how to protect our memory. Therefore, we all have some of Judas's attitudes, albeit unconsciously.

Who isn't a betrayer? Perhaps you have never betrayed someone else, but you have surely betrayed yourself and your own quality of life.

How many times have you told yourself that you would be more patient, but an offense made you angry? You betrayed your intention.

How many times have you promised that you would love more, smile more, live more peacefully, work less, worry less—but haven't kept your promise? Some betray their sleep while others betray their dreams.

Our model of thinking correctly has a lot to teach us about putting our minds to work, if only we will become his apprentice.

---

*Thinking Correctly to Manage Your Memory:*
# The dream that became a nightmare

João Paulo was a young man from a simple background who lived in a small town. His parents owned a small shop.

He had always been a brilliant student who efficiently assimilated information, was dedicated to his schooling, and was praised by his teachers and friends because of his grades. João Paulo dreamed of becoming a doctor and wanted to get into the best schools so that he could relieve the pain of others and make a real contribution to society. His voice resounded with passion when he talked about being a medical student.

Because of his background, few people believed that he'd get into medical school, but he had a dream—a life project—and not just the superficial intentions of desire that can't handle the high temperatures of difficulty. His dream was so strong that it resisted the heat of adversity and motivated him to study for several hours each day, as well as to improve his intellectual prowess. He studied hard and, in the end, performed excellently in his schoolwork. When he found out that he had passed, he jumped around like a child and felt deeply accomplished. His friends threw him parties. His parents couldn't control their joy. They were proud of their son who, despite not having studied at the best schools, had gotten into not just a medical school, but one of the finest in Brazil.

João Paulo had no idea that he would soon face psychological avalanches that would threaten to bury him completely.

During his first year, he did extremely well academically. Learning of each bodily organ and its mysterious functions was a great adventure for João Paulo. He studied cellular microbiology and found another world within those more than two trillion cells that comprise the human body. He'd study tissue, another unknown universe, and it excited him. Indeed, medicine enchanted him.

However, it didn't take long for his dream to become a huge nightmare. He, like most people, was unaware of the traps that can be laid in the vault of intelligence: our memory. He was unaware of certain basic phenomena within this patchwork of the personality. But he was soon to find out.

One time he studied very hard for an exam, knowing that he needed a good grade and that the professor didn't like him. On the day of the exam, he became so anxious that he blocked his intelligence with an anxiety that closed the windows of his memory. As a result, he couldn't recall anything that he had studied.

Not only did he do terribly on the exam, but he had been betrayed by his own insecurity and fear. This experience robbed him of sleep. He couldn't understand why he'd been unable to answer questions that he knew the answers to. Yet instead of trying to overcome the reality, he grew troubled.

The more he thought about it, the more his anxiety expanded. He subtly began to fear that this blockage might repeat itself during other exams. And it did. He studied very hard for his next test, but when he took it, he recalled his previous failure and became upset. He fell into the same trap that had been set up in the backstage of his mind. The volume of his anxiety increased so much during the exam that he blocked countless memory windows, making it difficult to rescue the information that he was perfectly familiar with.

When emotional tension is great, it blocks the *Homo sapiens* and sets the *Homo bios*—what I call our animal-like instincts—free. In other words, as our mind focuses on tension, that which makes us human (our capacity to think) becomes diminished, and our biology, our instincts, kick in. That is why, as I've said, our most foolish reactions occur during the first thirty seconds of anxiety.

This was the beginning of the assault on João Paulo's mind. His performance began to be compromised in most of the exams he took. His self-esteem evaporated. And each failure was given privileged status in his memory by the automatic memory registry, generating killer windows and zones of conflict.

When he was facing similar stimuli, which in his case were new exams, the memory trigger was fired in thousandths of a second, opening these unhealthy zones. They were read without the authorization of his "self," and the drama of the previous failures was reproduced on the stage of his mind—generating yet another high peak of anxiety, which in turn blocked the memory windows that contained the information he had learned. It was a psychodynamic cycle that disabled him intellectually.

This process is the same one that generates several phobias and causes the most intellectual performance deficits. João Paulo blocked 80 to 90 percent of his memory during his exams. Many people don't block such a high percentage, but almost all of us block 10, 20, 30, or 40 percent of what we've recently assimilated.

Taking exams was no longer a simple test of João Paulo's knowledge. It had become a source of anguish. Thousands of young people go through the same struggle without their teachers knowing about it.

Outside of the exam rooms, João Paulo had a great capacity to take in, process, and debate information, but when taking an exam, his gifted mind became blocked. His professors couldn't understand what was happening to him. They didn't know the roles of memory and the complex labyrinth in which his mind worked, so they started judging him solely on his performance and branded him as irresponsible and lazy. And João Paulo failed his second year.

During his third year, his drama not only repeated itself but got worse. João Paulo studied hard and, since he knew the material well, he taught his classmates. But when he took his exams, he had to face the disturbing "blank," and suddenly it would again be as if he knew nothing.

Since he felt inhibited and inferior, he was unable to undo the perception his professors had of him. No one believed this young man. Not one professor spent time with him to enter into his world. (When we value knowledge more than the disciple, serious accidents happen. Students who get bad grades should receive special attention from their teachers. Within them might lie great thinking that could change the course of science and history. Remember Einstein. Unfortunately, many "Einsteins" get lost along the way.) Ironically, the medical school—that promoter of health—triggered João Paulo's illness. He went through another despairing year and flunked again. His agony only increased with the passing years. His failures continued, and the zones of conflict increased immensely, reaching various areas of his personality and making him ill.

The blocking mechanisms of João Paulo's mind were protecting him from what they perceived as situations of risk. Even though he wasn't really at risk, his anxiety shut down his memory, signaling to his brain that it was more important to react—to flee—than to think. To his mind, it was as if he were facing a poisonous snake in the jungle. The zones of conflict in his mind produced warnings of a constant threat, as if his life were at risk, even if the threat only existed inside of him.

Millions of people experience tachycardia, an increase in their breathing rate, and other psychosomatic symptoms as their bodies attempt to provide more oxygen and nutrients to escape their "enemies." What enemies?

Their bosses, their coworkers, their preoccupations, their insecurities—whatever enemies are constructed within their minds. Unfortunately, to this day there are many mental health professionals and academics who haven't had the opportunity of studying the complex roles of memory and, therefore, are unaware that it can easily be blocked by anxiety, a phobic reaction, social pressure, offenses, disappointments, frustration, loss, and even ecstatic or intensely positive emotions.

Since João Paulo didn't know how to reedit his unconscious movie, his protection mechanisms were being constantly triggered. They closed the paradise of conscious memory and opened the gates of unconscious anxiety. The young dreamer failed year after year, and his classmates couldn't understand what was happening to him. No one stepped up to help him; no one knew how to help him. All of the students who studied with him got good grades, but not him. Imagine what this young man's self-esteem was like. Imagine the tears he cried. Think of the feelings of guilt and self-criticism that circulated within the territory of his emotions.

After seven years of failing grades, João Paulo was finally asked to leave the school. This place that had been an arboretum of science had become a desert of injustice. The school had kicked out a brilliant young man without understanding the obstacles that obstructed his intelligence, without helping him to overcome his conflicts.

After he was kicked out, João Paulo developed a depressive crisis. That's when he came to me. Though he was deeply saddened and had no courage to continue exploring the labyrinths of his life, I realized, after analyzing his story, that he had excellent thinking skills and that his mind had great potential. He brought several poems he had written. All of them had literary finesse; he distilled wisdom in his words.

As I became familiar with his story, I couldn't pity him; I needed to encourage him and guide him toward transforming his failure into beautiful life lessons. But how could I do this? Sometimes we can analyze all the conscious and unconscious causes that have produced someone's conflicts, but it's not always enough to encourage him or her to reorganize, overcome, and rebuild. A person will say something like, "I understand the causes of my car accident, but what do I do with my broken bones?" That's why, in my opinion, it is necessary to join the analysis of the facts with the correction of the facts; join the understanding of the causes that generate psychic illnesses with cognitive action on their dynamics.

During our time together, I explained some of the phenomena that are at the core of the workings of the mind and a few relevant roles of memory, exactly like I'm doing in this book. I noticed that João Paulo understood everything easily. Gradually, a light shone within his mind when he began to understand how his fear and anxiety had obstructed his memory.

Once he understood how the art of thinking can crumble, he recognized that his problem was not a weak intellect but that he was the victim of hidden psychological traps. His terrible performance on exams was his mind's way of protecting him, but that self-protective mechanism had backfired and sabotaged his success.

He successfully used the DCD technique, and the result was fascinating. A young man who might have gone through life shackled by an unwarranted inferiority complex, low self-esteem, and labels of incapacity began to produce again and became a professional journalist who excels to this day.

## Suggested Topics for Reflection and Discussion

1. We need to know the various roles memory plays to successfully protect the secrets of our personality and filter stressful stimuli. Which role of memory has impressed you the most?
2. The registry of memory is automatic, realized through the AMR phenomenon. Everything that happens in the theater of your mind is automatically recorded there. Every day, you either plant flowers or accumulate rubble in your memory. Did you know that? Have you concerned yourself with what is registered in your memory?
3. The emotion determines the quality of the registry. Experiences with

greater degrees of tension are registered in a privileged manner. Do you try to work through your anger, anxiety, and frustration to protect your memory?

4. Memory cannot be deleted, only reedited. Do you reedit the movie of your unconscious, doubting your negative thoughts, criticizing your anxious reactions, and determining that you will be free? Or do you passively wait for your crises to go away?

5. Jesus never gave up on anyone. He gave every chance to those who made mistakes, failed, betrayed, denied, or ignored their quality of life. Do you give yourself new chances? Do you know how to start over again? Do you invest in those who disappoint you?

## EXERCISES AND REMINDERS FOR DAILY PRACTICE

1. Referencing the characteristics of Principle #4—"Protect your memory"—described in the beginning of this chapter, journal about the ones you need to develop.

2. Record in your journal whether you filter stressful stimuli and protect your memory, or whether you allow small things to cause disturbances and anxiety.

3. Remember that one Think Correctly principle depends on and reinforces the other, so contemplate beauty and free your creativity even as you manage your thoughts and protect your emotions.

4. Act on the traumas, conflicts, and internal difficulties that you are aware of, using the DCD technique. Reedit the movie of your unconscious. Open the healthy windows in your memory.

5. Do not be passive in the face of emotional ideas and reactions that disturb you. Face and rethink your anxiety, relational concerns, activities, mental images, and unhealthy thoughts. Be the author of your story. This is your great goal!

## CHAPTER FIVE

*Principle #5:*

# Learn to Listen and Dialogue

Unless you live totally alone, cut off from all human interaction, listening and dialoguing (which is different from mere speaking) is a requisite part of human existence—and it plays an important role in attaining the happiness and interpersonal success you seek. Treating both skills as an art is the proper mind-set. Here are some traits that will be evident when someone takes this Think Correctly principle to heart.

The art of listening is

1. emptying yourself to listen to what others have to say rather than what you want to hear;
2. putting yourself in the place of others and being aware of their pain and needs;
3. penetrating the heart and unveiling the causes of aggressiveness, timidity, anguish, and unusual behavior;
4. interpreting what words don't say and what images don't reveal;
5. having the sensitivity to respect actual tears and to recognize those tears that are yet to be shed.

The art of dialoguing is

1. talking honestly about yourself;
2. exchanging life experiences;
3. revealing the secrets of the heart;
4. being transparent and real; not faking feelings and intentions;
5. not being ashamed of your mistakes or afraid of your failures;
6. respecting the limits and difficulties of others; not giving superficial answers;
7. interpersonal exchange that promotes the meeting of two or more psychological worlds and dissipates loneliness.

## Being Real

The arts of listening and dialoguing are cultivated in the soil of trust, empathy, and free exchange. Where there's a lack of trust, excessive demands and controlling behavior rise up like weeds, choking the life out of these two precious commodities of the mind. The two qualities go hand in hand: those who don't learn how to listen will never learn how to dialogue; those who don't learn how to dialogue will never become good listeners.

On the other hand, people who master the arts of listening and dialoguing will become more generous, more tolerant, humbler and more secure. They will notice more of a balance in their lives. Their creativity will improve because they're opening themselves to others' ideas even as they blossom within. They will also be greater influences for good in the lives of others.

However, developing these skills involves more than we may initially realize. We're used to talking. But talking is not dialogue. Talking is producing words, emitting sounds, speaking of everyday things, and discussing external happenings. Dialoguing is more profound. It is giving of yourself and expounding on your own story. It means leaving the preface behind to get to know the most important chapters of the people close to us.

Dialoguing means allowing oneself to be known by spouse, children, coworkers, and friends. It means removing our social mask. It means crying, apologizing, and embracing without fear, lending a shoulder for others to cry on. It means recognizing that we are human beings and nothing else. It means being transparent about our weaknesses, sharing our fears, and unfolding the fabric of our traumas.

How much people know you reveals the level of dialogue you have with them. Don't complain if they don't understand you; rather, question if you have really learned the art of dialoguing. Most people don't know how to dialogue, only how to talk.

On the flip side of the coin, what we call listening is all too often an exercise in waiting for the moment when the other person pauses so we can jump in and say what we want to say, irrespective of what we have just heard. Like politicians on TV, if there is something we want to say instead of answering a question we are asked, we say it. Not only is that disrespectful, but it keeps the dialogue from progressing toward a meaningful resolution or conclusion. In reality, this isn't listening at all—it is just another form of talking.

Let's look at how these qualities of listening and dialoguing play out—for better or for worse—in some of our primary relationships.

## The Marriage Relationship

Most couples, somewhere during their marriage, will develop a serious crisis of affection because they haven't learned the arts of listening and dialogue. They know how to talk, but they don't know how to talk about themselves or to listen with their hearts. They talk about politics, money, and the theater, but they are silent about their own stories. They know how to listen to sounds, but not to the voice of emotion. They're bold enough to argue the facts, but they are afraid of sharing their own feelings. They live together for years, but they don't become the best of friends.

Think of your personality as a big house. Most husbands and wives know each other's living room, but that may be the extent of it. They know each other's flaws but not the most intimate areas of their being. They discuss problems, but they aren't co-explorers in the same adventure, partnering to discover new territories. They don't reveal their distresses, and they don't talk about their internal conflicts or difficulties.

Therefore, if you want to cultivate love, the best way is not by giving expensive gifts but by offering a priceless jewel: your own being. The art of listening refreshes the relationship, and the art of dialoguing nurtures love. These are universal laws on which the best relationships are based.

Those who wish to cultivate a mind that thinks correctly must have the courage to ask the person they love at least four important questions—not just once, but throughout their lives:

- When have I disappointed you?
- Which of my behaviors annoys you?
- What could I do to make you happier?
- How can I be a better friend?

Wonderful couples with wonderful beginnings too often have sad endings because they don't practice being friends and exchanging experiences. They are great at defending their points of view, but they rarely recognize their mistakes or admit their relational failures. Yet, really, who doesn't err? Who doesn't act foolishly? It's possible to win all the battles in the relationship but to lose love.

Why don't we dialogue about ourselves? Because we're afraid of being criticized, misunderstood, or ridiculed. We're afraid of the emotional war that starts once we tell the secrets of the heart and become transparent about real feelings. To dialogue, you must not be afraid of acknowledging your mistakes or be ashamed of yourself. To listen, you must not be afraid of what your spouse will say. Couples must be soul mates. One of the most relaxing things in a relationship is knowing that we aren't perfect and yet still recognizing that we need each other.

So whether you're newlyweds or you've been married for years, banter with each other. Dream together. Complain less. Notice the small gestures, and thank your spouse for the small things he or she does for you. Give flowers for no special reason. Dine at different places. Surprise one another with unexpected behavior. Free your creativity, and get out of your relational rut. Spontaneity can have fantastic results—like the time my wife "kidnapped" me on a Friday afternoon after a stressful week. She wanted me to rest, and so she booked a room in a nice hotel where we enjoyed a relaxing weekend. For those kinds of reasons, after twenty years, my wife is still my girlfriend. She talks with me, she listens well, and then she uses what she's learned to draw us closer.

## The Parent-Child Relationship

In my research I have observed seven habits of correctly thinking parents, some of which I will comment on here. Ordinary-minded parents, within their means, see to their children's needs. They throw them birthday parties; buy them shoes, clothes, and toys; and travel with them. Parents who think correctly, on the other hand, give their children something incomparably more valuable: they give them their story, their experiences, their tears, and their time. Parents who give their children "things" are remembered until the memory of the "thing" fades, but parents who give themselves to their children become unforgettable.

Have the courage, therefore, to dialogue with your children about the saddest days of your life. Have the boldness to tell them about your difficulties and past defeats. Talk about your adventures, your dreams, and the happiest moments you've experienced. Let them get to know you. Most children have barely even seen the living room of their parents' personalities, much less been privy to the back rooms where true personality actually lives.

Also, when you dialogue with your kids, don't go on and on about how they don't appreciate all that you've done for them. Remember the AMR phenomenon. Because your voice is so strong in their lives, and because your kids are still very impressionable, avoid at all costs the kind of criticism that leaves a toxic memory in their minds.

## The Teacher-Student Relationship

Along the same lines, if you're an educator, don't be one who criticizes the mistakes of your students, who makes fun of their anxieties, or who goes on and on about how kids don't ever amount to anything. It won't get you positive results. Instead, seek to register an excellent image of you within them so that you can educate them.

A teacher who thinks correctly strives to enchant students every day. So don't be afraid to say things you've never said before—or to use a new method. Praise more and criticize less. Exalt small improvements. Ask students about their dreams and fears. This level of dialogue derails suicide attempts, overcomes trauma, and opens avenues for helping them celebrate life. (All of this is good advice for moms and dads too!)

And for both educators and parents, if you make a mistake, admit it in front of your kids—and apologize. Rather than diminishing your authority, this one gesture will establish the kind of authority that is built on reality and respect and that promotes teachability in the younger generation.

# Dependency and the Lessons of Life

The lower a species' form of life, the less it depends on its parents. In mammals—a higher life form—the young depend greatly on their parents to learn survival skills. In the human species this dependency is multiplied several times over. For example, a seven-year-old child is very immature and dependent, while many mammals of the same age are already close to death. Why? Because the learned experiences are more important than the instinctive ones.

Unfortunately, the typical modern family has become a group of strangers. Parents and children breathe the same air and eat the same food but aren't truly listening and dialoguing. There's no mutual learning of each other's life lessons. The family members are close physically but distant internally. Consequently, children are left to pick up random tips about living from observing their parents, rather than learning the "whys" and "wherefores" through dialogue. And when this happens, kids are far more susceptible to the influence of others outside the home, be that their peers or adults who might not have their best interests in mind.

The same process has been happening in schools. In my book *Brilliant Parents, Fascinating Teachers*, I state that education around the world is in crisis. Educators are unaware of the roles of memory mentioned in this book, so they don't develop adequate tools to shape thinkers. Children's memory banks are considered nothing more than depositories for information, so they are given loads of facts that do nothing to elevate their lives; the facts only diminish the joy of learning and build anxiety.

The classroom has become a gathering place of strangers who coexist without really relating to each other. Education simply has to be humanized so that teachers and students can blend their stories and students can learn life lessons within the classroom. The teacher who will talk about his or her world while talking about current events and academic subjects makes this a reality.

When this doesn't happen, students ultimately leave with diplomas in hand but unprepared in their hearts to deal with failure, disappointments, and challenges. They don't know how to open the windows of their mind, free their creativity, or think before reacting. They have not learned how to rescue the leader within.

If you wish to have students who don't frustrate you, children who don't disappoint you—and even coworkers who don't annoy you— you'd better move to another planet. Or you can learn to accept people, limitations and all, and build healthy relationships with them. And here's a tip that will greatly improve your ability to dialogue: never critique people until you've affirmed them. Many times I've erred by first pointing out the mistakes of others, including my own dear daughters. Fortunately, I've learned that first we must compliment—conquer the territory of emotion. Then we will be able to conquer the territory of reason and teach people something.

Memorize this pearl as well if you want to transform the relationship you have with those you love into a great adventure: an intelligent person learns from his or her mistakes; a wise person also learns from the mistakes of others.

## How Our Model for Thinking Correctly Listened to and Dialogued with Others

It has been my observation over the years that religious leaders— priests, pastors, rabbis, imams, monks—for all their spiritual guidance, do no more sharing of themselves than those to whom they preach. That's not a criticism, just an observation of the reality of their humanity and of their own need to learn the art of dialogue.

Did you know that religious leaders have as many secrets and wounds as anyone else? They experience the same conflicts and depressive moments, the same tendencies toward criticizing or alienating others, and the same fears of being misunderstood. They have genuine desires to serve their God faithfully and to do good in this world, but they tend to get put on a pedestal by their flock and thus become isolated—held to a standard of perfection that they know they can't possibly meet. In order not to deflate the expectations of those who hold them in such high esteem, they live a double life, just like regular people. They don't have anyone to whom they can express the true story of their lives. They talk about everything except themselves.

But it is not just religious leaders who keep the stories of their lives to themselves. Leaders in business, politics, government—leaders in all levels of society—live with the pressure of not revealing who they really are for fear of disappointing those they lead. They are controlled by the fear of what others will think and say about them.

Jesus, as a model of thinking correctly, did not live this way. He was completely free to dialogue about his own life—as we saw him reveal his anguish in the Garden of Gethsemane—without fear of judgment from others. He did not hesitate to let others in on his emotional state or to ask for the prayer support of his friends who were with him. It was to three fragile friends—Peter, James, and John, who would soon desert him in his most painful hour—that he exposed his intense spiritual conflict and suffering.[1] He was an admirable teacher in even this way.

Jesus could have shown his followers heroism and strength on the eve of his death, but he chose honesty and vulnerability instead. He chose to teach them that interdependency is the rule of life, that we need to be comforted and encouraged by each other. He demonstrated that to have quality of life we need to be human beings and not heroes. Barriers need to be broken down and gaps closed between pretense and reality.

The strongest person ever to walk on this earth cried his tears without fear. He allowed himself to be known. He was transparent. The AMR phenomenon in his disciples' unconscious registered an excellent image of him so that, even after his death, they learned to follow his example in any situation they faced. They understood that they also would go through crises and would need to face them and share them with others. It was Jesus' actions, not his lectures, that taught them about having an extraordinary life by thinking correctly.

Some people take their own lives because they don't have the courage, or the opportunity, to open up their hearts to other people. Others have their dreams crushed, their hopes torn apart, and their creativity shredded because they haven't discovered how to blend their stories with those of others. Their fear of criticism has caused them to live isolated within themselves—behaviors that have blocked their minds' potential and have stolen both their creativity and their inspiration.

Modern societies live at a superficial level as a result of not employing the skills of listening and dialogue. People wear disguises that mask who they really are. The only way to take the mask off is to tell people who we are and listen as others do the same.

## A Model of Listening and Dialogue

We are the only generation in history that has managed to destroy the younger generation's capacity to dream. In past generations, young people criticized social mores and dreamed of great accomplishments. Where are the dreams of youth now? Where are their questions?

Our aggressive society has lulled youth into passivity, taking away their identity and giving them an ID number instead. Rather than criticizing the poison of consumerism and the madness of immediate pleasure, young people have become servants to them. Our youth feel the future is unimportant. They have no cause or dream for which to fight or in which to invest. Parents and teachers should be the salespersons of dreams. They should plant the seed of beautiful dreams in the minds of the young to make them intellectually free and emotionally brilliant.

Jesus was an accomplished purveyor of dreams, inspiring those who followed him to dream of accomplishments on a global scale and motivating them to go into all the world and preach his gospel of love and redemption. He lifted up humanity and caused others to think of themselves in noble terms. In fact, he referred to himself as the "Son of Man," a reference to the value he placed on his own human nature. It was as the Son of Man that he sought to identify with the human beings he met who were needy in so many ways.

I have never studied anyone who loved life as much as Jesus of Nazareth did. Most humans love the things life provides, such as money, home, status, cars, and material comfort. Jesus, on the other hand, loved life itself—thinking, dreaming, creating, dialoguing, and listening. He was proud to be a human being, and he was intent on helping others experience an internally extraordinary life: "I have come that they may have life, and have it to the full."[2]

When people were around Jesus, the calloused became enchanted with life, the aggressive were calmed, and the illiterate came up with new ideas. Jesus patiently listened to the unreasonable things his disciples and others said and slowly began to challenge their worldview. During the Last Supper, when he might have justifiably been withdrawn and discouraged, he entered into profound dialogues with his disciples on what was about to happen. In spite of his impending death, he poured life into those he knew would be temporarily discouraged with the turn of events. He gave them reasons to hope. He taught them lessons of leadership and service by washing their feet, taking on the role of a servant.

Jesus loved to dialogue, to ask questions of those who were questioning him. He delighted in the prospect of expanding their minds and giving them a new vision. He saw the work of art contained in every piece of human marble and sought to shape it. He planted seeds with every contact, every appointment, and waited patiently for the harvest. He wanted to inspire his disciples' ordinary minds to think correctly—to aspire to inventiveness, to serenity, and to a transparency that would encourage deep relationships.

## Following the Model

Perhaps one of the biggest challenges for a member of modern society is to exercise the self-control that dialogue and listening require. True conversation is like a tennis match—the ball, the topic, must continually go back and forth in order for meaning to be maximized. There can be no game, no dialogue, if one person insists on serving every shot. But if we learn to give focused answers and offer brief comments so as to allow the back-and-forth of dialogue to continue, as Jesus did, our conversations and our relationships will be enriched.

---

*Think Correctly to Learn to Listen and Dialogue:*
# A hero in a wheelchair

Henrique was a thirty-eight-year-old man who had enormous scars that deformed his face. He was also a wheelchair-bound paraplegic. But most importantly, Henrique was a loving father to fourteen-year-old Tiago, and a gentle husband to his wife.

Because of his facial deformities, whenever Henrique arrived at any social gathering, conversation would stop and people would stare in shock. Tiago was extremely ashamed of people's reaction to his father's mutilated appearance, so much so that the boy had grown up trying to hide him. He wouldn't invite his friends over to his house, and he never invited his father to attend school functions. He also didn't talk to his father. They lived in the same house but in different worlds. The father had a secret, too, that the son had never heard. The price they paid for their silence was high. There was no closeness nor exchange of experiences in this small family.

Henrique was aware of his son's embarrassment, but despite how it hurt him, he would say nothing. This went on for years until the day Tiago caught the flu and stayed home from school. On that day, his teacher had given her students a group assignment that was to be handed in the following day. It would be a battle against the clock. Tiago's group was concerned about the deadline and showed up at his house unannounced. His mother greeted them and led them into the living room, then went to get Tiago in his bedroom.

Suddenly, Henrique rolled into the living room in his wheelchair. The students were shaken at the sight of him. At that moment Tiago came into the living room and saw that his friends were staring at his father's face. He was mortified.

But Henrique sought to ease the moment: "Don't worry, I know that I'm not good-looking!" he joked.

Tiago's classmates smiled and relaxed, but not Tiago. He wanted to run from the room, but he couldn't. Something kept him there.

Like many children, Tiago was so used to seeing his father's outer defects that he had never seen his inner qualities. He was unable to see the beauty hidden behind his father's scars. But his friends were seeing the sweetness of a man who had been mutilated by life.

Suddenly one of the students asked Henrique the question Tiago had always dreaded, "Why are you in a wheelchair, and how did you get those scars?"

Tiago blushed and wished he could hide under the couch. Henrique and his wife had always kept it secret, so Tiago had no idea what the answer would be.

The couple knew that one day they would have to tell their son the truth, and lately they had been commenting that it was time that Tiago knew the truth, but they hadn't decided when. Was this the moment?

Both parents looked at each other. The mother nodded, encouraging Henrique to share one of the most important chapters of his story. With a constricted voice Henrique turned to Tiago and said, "My son, when you were ten months old, we went to visit a beautiful hotel on a farm. Your mother and I took a long walk and left you with the nanny. Thirty minutes later we saw smoke coming from the direction of the hotel."

After a deep sigh, Henrique continued, "We hurried back to the hotel, and as we came closer, we saw that it was burning. Desperately, we ran without stopping, looking for you until we were out of breath, but not finding you. When we saw the nanny alone, we panicked. She had abandoned you to go to the pool and was afraid of going back into the hotel to rescue you. There was a lot of confusion, and the building was near collapse."

Tiago was astonished with this story; he seemed to be watching the scenes as his father described them. "Profoundly afraid for you, I tried to rush into the hotel. Some people held me back and said that it was madness; they asked me to wait for the firemen to arrive. But . . . your life was more important than my own. I would risk anything to save you."

Tiago's eyes welled up. One of his friends embraced him in an attempt to comfort him. Henrique continued, "The heat was unbearable. I couldn't breathe. I cried out your name, but I couldn't find you. I'd go into the wrong rooms, and I couldn't see clearly where I was. Suddenly, I heard the weak coughing and crying of a baby. I ran toward the sound. It was you, my son. In the middle of all the smoke and fire, I had finally reached you. I grabbed you up in my arms and ran out of the hotel, but as I was running, I slipped on something. Yet I managed to protect you from the fall so that you didn't get hurt."

It was then that Tiago looked down and began to cry. Almost inaudibly Henrique added, "The firemen then took you from my arms and carried you out of harm's way. As I was getting up, a beam fell on my back and broke my spine, leaving my face exposed to the flames, and I was burned."

Henrique stopped the story to wipe his tears, and then he said with great sensitivity, "I know that people are disturbed because of my face. But the scars that shake them are the same ones that cry out that I love you, Tiago, and that bear witness that if necessary, I would do it again because of the love I feel for you. I'm sorry, Son, that I'm not like other fathers—a handsome person who can play and run like they do."

For the first time, father and son were brought together through dialogue. Crying in a loud, shaky voice, Tiago said, "Why haven't you told me this story before? Why?"

His question generated a prolonged moment of silence between them while Tiago searched inside himself. The art of dialogue had illuminated the areas of his mind that had been blocked, especially his ability to put himself in the place of others and see the invisible. For the first time he saw that behind his father's scars was an extraordinary man, a man he didn't know. If he had once felt ashamed of his father's deformed face, now he was ashamed of his selfishness and prejudice.

Crying, he asked once again, "Why did you keep this story from me?"

Henrique answered, "Your mother and I decided not to tell you the story until now so that you'd never feel that because of you I was paralyzed and deformed. I was afraid that if you knew, you'd grow up feeling guilty or wouldn't do so well at school out of pity for me. If I was wrong, I apologize."

Like Henrique, so many times when we try to do right, we make mistakes. We hide the most important chapters of our lives to spare our children. But how can we teach them to cry their tears if we hold back our own? How can we encourage them to maturely work through their wounds if we are silent about our own?

Within minutes the acts of dialoguing and listening reedited some killer windows in Henrique and Tiago's relationship, windows that had kept them apart. Not all of the windows were reedited—it would take months and even years to achieve such a process. But what's important is that dialogue and listening began to build parallel positive windows that would open the way to a new relationship.

Tiago recalled his attitude of trying to hide his father from his friends. He then looked into his father's eyes, and as if he could see the core of his heart, he said, "Father, I'm the one who should apologize. I didn't know that underneath the person in a wheelchair was a hero who loved me and fought for me through it all."

Tiago then ran into his father's arms. It was the first time that he had given him such an emotional hug. He then did something that his father never imagined he would do: Tiago kissed Henrique's scars. They were no longer causes of shame but of pride.

From that moment on, father and son became great friends and wrote a new story. The AMR phenomenon "painted" a beautiful picture in each person's unconscious that made a lasting conscious impression, and that became the foundation of a rich relationship.

Unfortunately, millions of parents and their children know how to talk about anything except themselves. They know each other's scars but not their hearts—their dreams, adventures, tears, fears, failures, and their life projects. At best, they know the living room of each other's personality. They are foreigners living in the same land.

The art of listening and dialoguing deeply in an open, sincere manner saturated with love and respect cures the relational wounds that thousands of criticisms can't. The art of listening and dialoguing makes us understand and not judge, accept and not point out flaws, enter into deeper layers of the personality and not just skim the surface.

Henrique and Tiago's story illustrates an amazing fact: an ordinary mind learns how to speak of the world it lives in, but a correctly thinking mind learns to speak about the world we are.

### Suggested Topics for Reflection and Discussion

1. The art of listening is the capacity to listen without prejudice. When you listen to someone, do you try to put yourself in that individual's place, or do you listen to what you want to hear?
2. The art of dialoguing is the art of talking about yourself and exchanging life experiences. Are you afraid of talking about yourself? Are you afraid of being criticized, judged, or misunderstood?
3. How is your marriage relationship? Have you been an open book to your loved one? Are there fewer compliments and more criticism? Have you used small gestures to enchant your spouse?
4. How is your relationship with your children? Do you criticize them a lot? Have you shared your story with them? Have you stopped to listen to them, gotten to know their dreams, their fears, their disappointments? Do they know you? Do they know your goals, successes, failures, and tears?
5. Jesus wasn't ashamed of talking about himself; he wasn't afraid of his anguish. Is there an emotional pain or conflict that you would like to talk about but haven't been able to?

### Exercises and Reminders for Daily Practice

1. Referencing the characteristics of Principle #5—"Develop the art of listening and dialoguing"—described in the beginning of this chapter, journal about which ones you need to develop.
2. Journal about the quality of your dialogue with these six groups of people: parents, spouse, children, friends, students, coworkers. What grade would you give yourself? What grade would you give the transparency and listening in each group? Take into account how well you

know each other, whether you exchange experiences, and the frequency of your dialogue.

3. Turn off the TV and invite your children, your spouse, or a friend to dialogue once a week. Every now and then, make a date with one of your children or your spouse and talk openly to each other. The best way to help a person to open up is to abandon your own pride and tell them your story.

4. Surprise those you love with small gestures. Lose your fear of crying, of apologizing, of telling them you love them and need them.

5. Practice putting yourself in the place of others and discerning what is behind their reactions and behavior. Listen more, judge less, and understand more.

6. Be spontaneous and transparent—be yourself—rather than worrying what others think and say about you and trying to conform to their perceptions.

## CHAPTER SIX

*Principle #6:*

# Learn the Art of Self-Dialogue

In the previous chapter we explored the arts of interpersonal dialogue and listening—communication with those closest to us. In this chapter we will look at another kind of dialogue, a deeper dialogue: the art of dialoguing with oneself. Self-dialogue, which I call "the roundtable of the self," is characterized by the following:

1. A fully aware, open internal dialogue and debate with one's "self"
2. A reunion with your personal life-story
3. Direct intervention in your traumas, conflicts, difficulties, and fears
4. Continual revision of goals and reevaluation of how you face life
5. The ability to decide, question, and direct your own story
6. Becoming your own best friend
7. Quieting your thoughts and calming your emotions

## More Than Talking to Yourself

In English we have the expression "mind over matter," but people aren't taught how to think correctly—how to dialogue internally in order to manage their thoughts, reorganize their emotions, recycle their fears, overcome their anxieties, work out their frustrations, and rewrite the stories that they are constructing in their memory. And yet learning and practicing this art expands some specific areas of the mind's potential, including your inventiveness, your safety, and your authenticity.

It's easy to be lulled into thinking that wisdom and maturity are measured by how many things a person owns, his academic prowess, or the level of his giftedness, but this is simply not so. Your wisdom and maturity are determined by your ability to have frequent and honest "roundtable discussions" with yourself for the purpose of questioning your thoughts and emotions, criticizing your beliefs, rethinking your life, and retracing your steps. Think of it as a board of directors meeting with yourself, where you are the chairman of the board who sets the agenda.

In these "discussions," we shouldn't only talk *about* our fears, conflicts, bad moods, intolerances, and insecurities—but talk *to* them. The correctly thinking person will be intimately acquainted with himself or herself and very comfortable with the ongoing process of self-evaluation via self-dialogue. Though there are many people who are not comfortable with solitude, if you are your own best friend, solitude becomes an opportunity for reflection, correction (if needed), and advancement in maturity.

Violating this principle of how to think correctly has contributed to the collective illness of modern society—not classical mental illnesses as catalogued by psychiatrists, but illness as evidenced by symptoms such as stress, ATS, emotional instability, loneliness, and the inability to converse intimately with others based on a lack of comfort with one's own self. It is impossible to be the author of your story, direct your thoughts, manage your emotions, and elevate your quality of life if you don't have the courage to intelligently debate your problems and review your paths within yourself.

The "self roundtable" is a step beyond the DCD technique, not only in its depth but in its duration. Many people go for years without an open, sincere dialogue with themselves. Some people are born, grow, and die without *ever* having a meaningful encounter with their own stories. They lived without having a romance with life. And that is a tragedy.

## A Species That Doesn't Respect Itself

Children spend in excess of ten years learning to speak their native language, but in that learning process they never develop the skills of sharing about themselves or conversing with themselves. Yet how can young people develop into mature adults if they don't know how to probe the deepest levels of their own being?

If Nazi soldiers during World War II had traveled to the center of their beings and had each held an internal roundtable discussion, questioning the propaganda they were being fed and their own participation in the events, perhaps they would have rebelled against putting millions of innocent people—including children—to death. Germany had one of the richest philosophical and intellectual traditions in history. Yet all her learning was not sufficient to protect an enormous segment of her population from being seduced by the ideas of a psychopathic leader named Adolf Hitler.

Because modern academia is not equipping students with the skills of internalization and critical conscience, the same thing could happen again. Only a critical "self" that has been taught how to debate with itself and consider its choices will be strong enough to withstand the pressures of external forces that promote evil.

While a lot is said about human rights in developed countries, what can be said of individual tolerance in the face of tension? For all of our progress and achievement as the human race, the tipping point at which we personally get angry is actually the lowest it's ever been. More primitive than sophisticated. For example, if you make a mistake in traffic, people flash aggressiveness instantly—they honk and throw obscene gestures (or worse). Such behavior is so common it even has a clinical name: road rage.

The sad irony is this: we will rage at being cut off in traffic but yawn over a multitude of true social injustices, such as racism, abortion, government ineptitude, the destruction of marriage and the family, amoral educational systems, and the like. The fact that people lose their patience over trivial and meaningless things without a thought toward serious crimes against humanity is evidence that we've been taught no internal system of management that directs our emotions toward appropriate objects and in appropriate directions.

Emotional time bombs are exploding all around us too, especially among the young. Random shootings on campuses, teenage suicide, murder rates, terrorist attacks—all these are signs of a species in crisis, a species that misunderstands its mind and misperceives its more important characteristics. These bombs will continue to go off if they are not disarmed by people getting in touch with who they are.

## Humanizing Ourselves—Journeying Inside

Talking to yourself sounds like an insane proposition, but it's not. What is truly insane (or at least not normal) is the absence of intelligent self-dialogue. Those who put this Think Correctly principle of self-dialogue into practice not only have more means of overcoming their psychological suffering but also of humanizing themselves—of becoming more tolerant and serene and humbler—because they have recognized their limitations and weaknesses. They have a far more realistic view of themselves than those who don't self-dialogue, and therefore can protect themselves better on many levels.

The roundtable of the self pulls us from the throne of pride and self-sufficiency and seats us among our "peers," so to speak. But when we put ourselves on a pedestal—which is the logical outcome of the failure to self-dialogue—it is easy to judge and condemn. A person's greatness lies in his capacity to put himself in the place of others and understand what needs or weaknesses are at the root of her behavior. How is this empathy for others to be gained except through discovering and understanding oneself?

My own process of self-dialogue has made me aware that I have too many failings and limitations to be occupied with others' imperfections. You'll have the same perspective if you hold these meetings with yourself. When you understand how small and fallible you are, it is much easier to understand the failings and smallness of others.

I firmly believe that if modern-day terrorists practiced the roundtable of the self, they would never blow up their own bodies to destroy innocent people. They would understand that we aren't only Arabs, Jews, Americans, or members of rival religious sects, but members of a unique and priceless species. They would love more, empathize more, judge less. They would realize that the perceived injustices that spark their retaliations are the fruit of a species that doesn't see its mistakes.

Likewise, if those who are attacked practiced this technique, they would understand that, regardless of cultural and religious differences, their attackers are not alien flesh and blood; they have the same theater of the mind and the same type of thoughts as their victims. The two sides could then meet on some middle ground and embrace their similarities rather than flexing their military muscles.

A person that has the goal of expanding his or her mind must frequently conduct the roundtable of the self. Those who practice inner dialogue strengthen their capacity to be a leader of themselves and make decisions, understanding that every choice implies a loss. For example, it is not possible to choose peace without forfeiting revenge. But on the field of social conflict, those who are most aware of the greatness of life will willingly suffer more losses, lesser losses, to enjoy the great gains that come with an extraordinary life.

## How to Practice the Roundtable of the Self

The roundtable of the self isn't about simply producing thoughts within the silence of our minds; we all do that naturally—probably too much. Rather, it is thinking while creating an intimate debate. It can be used as a psychotherapeutic technique that heals the psyche and aids in overcoming anxiety, stress, and other disorders, or as a teaching technique that trains the psyche, turns us into thinkers, and prevents psychological illnesses.

The roundtable of the self acknowledges an internal society. It gathers the members within you—the cast of characters in the theater of your mind—and holds a meeting. And as in any society meeting, many items are discussed. In this case, your conscious "self" debates with your frustrations, crises, disturbances, life goals, and dreams, asking a series of questions: "Where? Why? How? When? What are the causes? Is this the right path or the wrong path? Is it worth it?"

For example, a man suffers a panic attack, afraid that he will suddenly die or lose consciousness. Now, he can either be controlled by the panic or debate it. If he holds a roundtable discussion about the problem, he will seriously criticize it, rethink it, and question it. He asks himself, "What is the logic behind my panic? When did it begin? Why did it begin? Why am I enslaved by it when I'm in excellent health? I demand to be free."

This principle of thinking correctly does not replace psychiatric treatment with medication or other forms of psychotherapy if they are needed. But it is a powerful complementary tool. Most people—indeed, many professional therapists—have no idea how powerful the "self" is. Many mental illnesses, including schizophrenia, appear precisely because the "self" isn't structured, isn't critical, and isn't its own leader. Once it becomes a puppet for fantasies, disturbing thoughts, and tense emotions, the self loses its identity and logic.

Consider a young college student I know who once struggled with insomnia. In his sleeplessness, his thoughts would accelerate and produce many illogical mental images. Since his "self" didn't question, criticize, or confront the images, he began to buy into them as if they were real. The young man who was once so full of potential let the characters in the theater of his mind play whatever roles they wanted, and he became confused and disoriented.

First he believed that he was a great artist. Then he began to think that he was the dictator of Iraq. In the end, he had a psychotic crisis that required medication to decelerate and organize his thoughts. During his treatment he learned how to doubt and criticize his thoughts, and he rescued his internal leader. He also learned to dialogue with himself, which not only prevented new crises but allowed him to eventually regain his sanity.

He is just one example of how deeply the art of self-dialogue affects our lives.

## How the Roundtable Affects the Memory Windows

The DCD technique should be applied especially when we're at the height of our insecurity, anxiety, or despair. In moments of extreme tension, deep reflection isn't possible; it's necessary to act quickly against the unhealthy thoughts that are attacking our peace and tranquillity. In contrast, the roundtable of the self should be in progress before we ever enter the arena of tension. If the roundtable is part of our lifestyle, then we can engage in self-dialogue with calm reflection, analyzing our relationships, conflicts, and challenges *before* they become crises.

As I have explained previously, the DCD technique reedits the unconscious movies in our mind. But the roundtable does more. It builds parallel windows in memory, creating new spaces for clear thinking. These phenomena are among the most important secrets of the workings of the mind. If you understand them, you will create paths that lead to a successful, healthy life.

Human memory is opened through millions of "windows" in the brain's cortex, each window containing thousands of pieces of collected information. Some windows generate pleasure, courage, and intelligent answers, while others are unhealthy, generating affliction, hatred, and emotional blockages. Sometimes a joy or sorrow will come to mind for no apparent reason because a particular window was opened arbitrarily.

Have you ever had that déjà vu feeling where you're sure you know a place you've never been before? This happens because of an external stimulus—in this case, the image of the place—which opens windows containing thousands of images of the past. Some of these images can contain traces of locations similar to the one you are viewing at present, producing the sensation of having visited it before.

Some people feel an incomprehensible sorrow at nightfall. But there is a good explanation for it. When their social rhythm diminishes at day's end, they internalize their feelings and subtly open the windows that contain past experiences of tedium and isolation. Thus, they construct an emotional experience of loneliness and sadness.

This entire game of opening and reading the memory windows is unconscious. Still, many types of unhealthy windows reside here: phobic windows that generate claustrophobia, social phobia, panic attacks, and the like; obsessive windows that generate fixed ideas; anticipatory windows that generate anxious thoughts about tomorrow; and low self-esteem and timidity windows that generate self-image disorders and excessive concern with the opinions of others. Depending on the volume of tension produced by a window (anger, hatred, anxiety), it can become a killer window—an area that drastically obstructs the reading of the other windows. When the positive windows are obstructed, reason is blocked during that moment.

This phenomenon explains why we are a species that can produce poetry and build unity among some people even while we are making wars and destroying and dominating other people without any rationality. It also explains our incoherent reactions and difficulties in leading our own selves.

## Killer Windows

How many times have we hurt those who deserve our understanding the most, or produced wounds that couldn't heal in just a matter of moments? How many times have we lost control of our reactions only to realize, after we've cooled off, that we could have dealt with things more calmly? How many parents, in a moment of frustration, have said what they should never say to their children? How many teachers have done the same in their classrooms?

These instances are all examples of killer windows at work. They block our minds and "assassinate" our reason and creativity, making us react instinctively, even ferociously—like animals. They destroy couples in love, longtime friendships, and professional relationships. We have to be on guard against killer windows and their effects if we're going to achieve the healthy lives and minds we're capable of.

As we've seen, some killer windows disable the minds of brilliant students. When they have an exam or interview, their level of anxiety is increased, which blocks the reading of the areas of memory containing the information they have learned. In other words, these destructive windows keep them from having access to the helpful memory windows. Hence, they perform poorly.

People who think correctly learn not to be the victims of this phenomenon by using the DCD technique and the roundtable of the self. Drastically doubting aggressive reactions, criticizing impulsivity, and determining to have self-control in moments of tension is an act of love for life that few practice. Not only would illnesses be prevented, but many relational conflicts would be avoided altogether, or resolved quickly when they arose.

Some psychiatrists don't use psychotherapy to treat panic syndromes and depression. Rather, they use medicines and medicines alone, because they overvalue the hypothesis that altering the serotonin levels and other substances within the brain is the best solution.

The use of medication can be important, but it is incomplete. We must fundamentally understand that psychological illnesses are produced by opening the windows of our memory on bad experiences. These negative windows lead to unhealthy chains of thoughts and emotions, such as negativity, self-destructive images, morbid ideas, and anguished fantasies that can control and enslave the self, making it a passive spectator of any number of disorders. Thus it is fundamental that even as you learn where the problems originate, you learn to rescue your inner leader through the techniques you are reading about. The "self" must go onstage and learn how to take the lead.

## Understanding the Power of Thinking Correctly

Those who are claustrophobic suddenly open a killer window when they enter an elevator. A few minutes earlier, they were on cloud nine; now they are in emotional hell. When they open the killer window containing the claustrophobia, they experience a sudden and dramatic fear that, transmitted to the cerebral cortex, will produce psychosomatic symptoms such as rapid heart rate, elevated blood pressure, excessive sweating, and increased respiration. They feel as if they can't breathe, as if they are about to die.

If they apply the DCD technique, they can stop being enslaved by their fear; register new, healthy experiences; and reedit the killer window. In other words, they can overcome their zones of conflict or trauma. If they are unable to apply the DCD technique, they should do the round-table of the self after the phobic crisis passes. What's the point of doing the roundtable after the crisis? To create parallel windows that will become linked to the unhealthy windows.

By asking a series of questions related to their fear and insecurity— for example: Why am I insecure? Why do I feel fearful? If I desire to be free, why does the fear control me? When did the fear start? What has triggered it? Are the origins of my fear and insecurity real or imaginary?— the claustrophobic person will create a series of experiences on the mind's stage that will be registered in the backstage of memory, creating healthier, parallel windows. This amazing process promotes psychological health and emotional freedom. Then, the next time that person enters an elevator, two things will happen simultaneously. A killer window will suddenly be opened in his or her memory, and the positive parallel windows will open too. This will strengthen the self and provide resources for self-direction out of the crisis.

These phenomena and techniques are applicable to all psychological and social disorders. It is impossible to erase the past, but it is possible to both reedit it and build parallel windows for the construction of a new view of the world and new experiences altogether.

Conducting the roundtable of the self is fundamental to thinking correctly. It's fundamental to stopping our passivity and conformity and to developing the capacity to make decisions, start over after we fail, and change our paths. Plenty of people perpetuate their troubles because they don't know how their minds work or how to help themselves. But if you will learn and practice these secrets, you will never view life or live it the same way again.

## How Our Model of Thinking Correctly Practiced the Art of Self-Dialogue

Jesus knew this to be true: it takes a person with a high quality of life to impart life to others. For that reason he was committed to correct thinking, and self-dialogue was a technique he used. He frequently isolated himself—intentionally leaving the crowds and his disciples and friends to retreat to an out-of-the-way place. Prayer was the primary focus of these retreats, a gateway to his self-dialogue and examination. His prayers were not religious, formatted, and systematic, but were free-form entries into his mind and spirit.

## Jesus Used the Roundtable of the "Self"

Once, a group of religious experts asked Jesus why his disciples didn't wash their hands before they ate bread (which was in violation of religious rituals of cleanliness).[1] Jesus was well aware of something his opponents were blind to: that humanity had never treated its true problems, had never dealt with the causes of social and psychological violence. So while Jesus considered hygiene and physical health important, the focus of his concern was mental health—dealing with the garbage that accumulates inside of human beings.

He saw the contradictions in people. They tried to rid themselves of their external filth but not of the invisible filth deposited in the psyche. They concerned themselves with their physical nourishment but not with the quality of ideas and emotions that nourished their personalities.

Understanding that a healthy person forms healthy people and a leader forms other leaders, Jesus gazed at the scribes and Pharisees and confronted them with their hypocrisy: for many of those who came near him and praised him with their mouths were far from him in their hearts. Contrary to what politicians crave, he didn't want admirers who expanded his popularity rating but people who upheld integrity in their lives. He didn't want slaves; he wanted the human heart to be whole and wholly free of deception.

To many people, applause is more than enough; to him, it was completely insufficient. Like a miner for gold, Jesus searched for human beings who knew themselves, who understood their failures and acted within themselves. He searched for people who thought correctly.

Jesus spoke this truth to those religious leaders: "It is not what goes into a man's mouth that makes him unclean, but what comes out of his mouth."[2]

When his disciples heard what he said to the leaders, they asked him, "Do you know that the Pharisees were offended when they heard this?"[3] They were concerned with the social implications of what Jesus said rather than with what concerned Jesus.

Jesus answered them with a parable to stimulate their imaginations:

"Every plant that my heavenly Father has not planted will be pulled up by the roots. Leave them; they are blind guides. If a blind man leads a blind man, both will fall into a pit."

Peter, never hesitant to speak up, said what the others were afraid to: "Explain the parable to us."[4]

And Jesus challenged their lack of perception: "Are you . . . still without understanding?"[5]

The disciples had been walking with Jesus for a long time but still had not grasped that mankind's problems are internal, not external. It is not just dirty hands that need to be changed but also tainted minds.

Jesus knew that until the human heart and the theater of the mind are made healthy, all the external conventions that we value so highly will only continue to create conflict. So he used questions and parables to jump-start his disciples' thinking: confronting their preconceptions, censoring their narrow and traditional ideas, and challenging them to make more mature choices. He wanted them to become thinkers—to become the lead actors on the stage in the theater of their minds and initiate a bold self-dialogue. In this case, he wanted them to see that evil springs from within, not without. Anger, impulsive reactions, discrimination, and fear come from the psychological heart of man. They not only create disturbances in the present, but they get rooted in the soil of memory by the automatic memory register, where they remain until the correctly thinking person tills the soil with new stimuli.

## A Few Words, an Entire Life

A few words can contaminate a life. Some people, when rejected, become blocked. Others use rejection as a trampoline for growth.

When an eleven-year-old child moved with her parents to an English-speaking country, she felt inferior and isolated herself because of her inability to speak the native language. Once, a teacher asked her a question in class that the little girl couldn't understand, and the teacher mocked the child in front of the whole class, causing the other students to laugh. Those few moments contaminated that little girl's memory and marked her—for a while.

The child who used to be so happy lost her smile; she became depressed, felt aversion for the teacher, and didn't want to return to school. Her father, realizing the gravity of the problem, helped her. He praised her, encouraged her, and entered into her world. Fortunately, she reedited her story without needing any treatment. If she hadn't overcome it, there might have been serious consequences.

Contrast her with the employee who was cruelly spoken to by an executive during a meeting. This employee had always done a brilliant job at the company, but he had failed in one project. So, demonstrating a failure to manage people and his own thoughts, the executive labeled the employee "incompetent" in front of his coworkers.

Humiliated, the employee registered the public embarrassment in a multidimensional way. He produced a killer window that blocked his memory. He was never able to shine after that and was ultimately fired. His subsequent depressive reactions and feelings of hatred for the executive required psychiatric treatment.

Then there are the high-achieving kids whose parents compare them to other kids and place unreasonable demands on them. The children try to compensate with exemplary performance in academics or athletics. In spite of the obvious upside, these kids might be setting themselves up for future failure if they don't learn to reedit their unconscious movie or create parallel windows when they face loss and challenges.

Jesus was fully aware of this process. He knew that we could contaminate the soil of memory and seriously jeopardize the development and fruit of the personality. He constantly conducted internal roundtables and searched every corner of his mind. He also searched the minds of other people. Only with such a foundation could he categorically say that our greatest enemies are within us. What comes out of us is what can destroy others and ourselves.

By inference, he meant that our failure to manage our thoughts, govern our emotions, and dialogue with ourselves has been the source of all human misery. To him, those who didn't think correctly and activate their inner leader would live an unhappy life and would contaminate others' memory windows, for it is from within that negative and destructive behaviors flow: everything from pessimistic, vicious, destructive, aggressive, rigid, discriminatory, and insensitive thoughts to adultery (betraying a loved one and betraying one's own conscience), theft (of objects, of the rights and freedom of others, and of quality of life), bearing false witness (injustice, distortions, corruption, and hidden intentions), and death (physical and emotional).

With the advance of medicine, we now can easily combat most infections. But how do we combat the contamination of memory? How do we rescue our inner leader if it is surrounded by unhealthy windows? How do we identify a killer window among the thousands of windows in our brains' cortexes?

Once memory is contaminated, the process is complicated. There are those who remain in psychotherapeutic treatment for years. There is no surgical or medical technology that can remove the killer windows. Fortunately, there is other relief available. We can use the two precious psychological tools that Jesus wielded with proficiency: the DCD technique and the roundtable of the self.

Practice them throughout your life, even if you don't have a psychological disorder, to enlarge the brilliant areas of your mind and to develop correct thinking. Do it spontaneously, in your own way, and according to your own intellectual capacity. Invest in your life. After all, life is a wonder waiting to be enjoyed.

## Following Our Model

Learning the art of self-dialogue will take discipline and practice, if for no other reason than that there are few moments in the average person's day that are devoid of mental intrusions. Setting aside time to self-dialogue—as Jesus did—is the ideal way, by intentionally removing oneself from social settings and entering solitude. With time, however, self-dialogue can become an ongoing part of life whenever it is needed and wherever time is available—while driving, during a bath, on a walk, or during lunch or work breaks.

---

*Thinking Correctly to Learn the Art of Self-Dialogue:*
# A man who lied to himself

A forty-five-year-old man, whom I will call Carlos, once came to see me. He was well-dressed, a Montblanc pen visible in his pocket. His movements were quick, and he expressed his ideas in a clear manner. Yet he couldn't hide the fact that he was suffocating inside at having to go through the most dramatic valley of frustration he'd ever encountered. His emotions lacked the "oxygen" they needed to breathe, and this produced all kinds of problems for him.

Carlos could not accept the things that were happening to him. He said he was losing the dearest people in his life: his wife and three children—an eighteen-year-old daughter, a seventeen-year-old son, and another daughter who was twelve. He told me that he had always fought for his family, that he'd worked very hard to give them an excellent life, sometimes putting in twelve hours a day at work. But his wife and children gave him no credit for it and seemed to hate him. They didn't value him or understand him, he said. They gave him neither affection nor empathy.

On the surface he appeared to be the person who had been treated unfairly, the unprotected victim within his family. However, as I began to treat him and enter into the maze of his story, I saw that underneath his apparent sweetness was the subtlest of tyrants.

It was true that his children couldn't stand him. It was also true that his wife wanted a divorce. But he had caused all of it. Carlos had made his family suffer intensely. He wasn't the type who attacked physically, and he wasn't aggressive with words, but he attacked people's emotions in a subtle and incisive fashion that few could withstand. Those who talked to him were charmed at first, but anyone who grew close to him ended up being intensely disappointed.

His wife and children never knew where they stood in their relationship with him. In fact, they didn't know who he was because Carlos was a specialist at lying, manipulating, and disguising his feelings and hiding his intentions. He lied all the time.

For example, when his children would ask him for something, he'd immediately say yes, giving no thought to the dynamics of his decision. He didn't consider whether or not he would have the money to buy it; he just always said yes. But in reality, his yeses were noes because his kids never knew what they'd get. Sometimes he would give them anything they wanted, making it seem as if money were no issue; the next moment he'd claim he couldn't keep up with the household bills, and he'd break his word.

Carlos wasn't aware that saying no might sting for a moment but is a wound that heals quickly and generates maturity. Saying yes and then not following through, on the other hand, generates distrust and the loss of empathy and respect. His children had a father who talked plenty and promised the world, but they didn't trust him or admire him.

There was no sense of security in that home either. His wife walked on quicksand. She never knew when they would sink financially, but she knew that sooner or later they would because this was part of the family's routine. Carlos didn't know how to have an open and honest dialogue with himself, and therefore he didn't know how to make consistent decisions and correct his ways. He personified the reality that a person with an ordinary mind talks with everyone, but a person who develops a mind that thinks correctly goes beyond and also talks to him- or herself.

Serious psychological and social problems, which can be solved, are perpetuated for years and sometimes are taken to the grave because of the lack of self-dialogue. Carlos deluded himself and deceived others. He was so manipulative that he believed his own lies and created his own reality. For example, it was typical of him to be in crisis for a while; then he'd switch to being abnormally ecstatic. One month he'd be completely defeated; the next, he'd give everyone the impression that he was soon to hit the jackpot. He was intelligent and sometimes did make a lot of money, but he never saved it; he had a compulsive need to buy.

There are people who cannot have a lot of money; they don't know how to think about the future and manage their assets for a rainy day. They believe that their success will be eternal and that their money will be endless. They're convinced that the future will always be a placid lagoon without waves. They don't acknowledge that life is full of surprises, and that sometimes we're at the top and sometimes we completely fail. They don't know that it is very difficult to be successful for more than five years straight, or to live without tribulation for five years. The unexpected always happens.

In Carlos's story, the unexpected happened every month, sometimes every week. He had the incessant desire to show his greatness and to be admired socially. The visibility of his Montblanc pen exemplified his neurotic need to show outer success, but the state of his family quietly testified of his failure to regard his inner condition. While he was talking his life away in his fine clothes and expensive cars, people were knocking at his door to collect overdue payments. Lawyers who represented his creditors frequently pressured him.

Finally, his wife could no longer stand living with a man who only sold illusions—a man who was hiding from himself. She preferred a simpler life, even if it meant paying her own rent and living paycheck to paycheck. That was better than living like a pendulum between heaven and hell.

There were reasons for Carlos's sick behaviors. He had gone through a tough time in his childhood. His father, a large man, would humiliate him in public and demand things that Carlos couldn't do. Like the time when Carlos was eight. His father was fixing the roof and asked the boy to bring up his toolbox, which weighed about forty pounds. Carlos couldn't physically do it, so his father beat him and said that he wouldn't amount to anything in life. Such behavior was typical. He would also arrive home drunk and beat Carlos's mother, and Carlos could do nothing to defend her. His father, who was a cop, had once even handcuffed a criminal to their porch and left him there all night. This truly shocked the boy.

The lesson here that I always like to emphasize is that underneath someone who hurts others is always someone who hurts. Understanding this relieves and protects us because it reduces our expectations toward others. Carlos's family was unaware of his story and expected too much from someone who could give very little.

Despite understanding Carlos's past and what was at the foundation of his reactions, I had to be honest with him: I told him that he would lose everyone who came into his life if he insisted on perpetuating his unhealthy lifestyle. He apparently loved his family, but his love was toxic. I told him that love grows in the terrain of admiration and trust. When admiration and trust are shaken, love begins to crumble.

To reverse course, he was advised that he could demand nothing from his children. Besides being unfair to them, any demand would drive them even further away. He would also have to learn how to be a transparent person. Instead of demanding attention, affection, tenderness, and understanding with his words, he would need to win them over with kindness. He'd have to learn the prayer of the wise: silence. However, before anything else, the person he had to win over was himself.

Carlos needed a roundtable with his own being. He needed to practice self-dialogue on a daily basis. Only he could find himself and ask who he was, what he wanted from life, what he expected from life, what people expected of him, and what were the consequences of his behavior. He was an anxious man who lived externally and who tried to escape from himself. He had no psychic comfort or internal peace. Therefore Carlos, like many people, had never achieved emotional rest despite the fact that he lived in a comfortable home.

It would be a difficult task, and many times painful, but if Carlos wanted to win anyone over, he would need to understand that his self was malformed, immature, superficial, manipulative, deceitful, unstable, and subtly aggressive.

Carlos began to analyze all of his behaviors. He inventoried his manipulations, lies, and false promises, along with his unhealthy need to be in the spotlight socially. He learned that those who need to do a lot to be socially appreciated don't appreciate and love themselves—and recognized himself in that truth. He conducted his roundtable every day, and not for ten minutes but sometimes for hours. Through the art of self-dialogue, his "self" became a close friend of the art of doubt, criticism, and determination, constructing a platform of consistent change in his mind.

I've rarely seen a man cry so hard. I've rarely seen someone become so frustrated with himself and, at the same time, have such a desire to rebuild his own story. His training paid off. The therapeutic dialogue, and especially his self-dialogue, encouraged him to reconstruct his shattered personality. Month after month he strengthened the greatest areas of his mind. In fact, he took such a gigantic step toward improving his quality of life that he apologized several times and in different ways to his wife and children. He had lost his fear of being who he truly was and abandoned the image of an unreachable man.

He went so far as to demonstrate what for him was a previously unheard-of humility: he declared his weaknesses and cried in front of his family. In the end, he didn't need to beg for their affection to win them over; he had only to reveal who he really was. There was an admirable man underneath that man who had lied to himself and his family. Fortunately, Carlos discovered this before it was too late.

## SUGGESTED TOPICS FOR REFLECTION AND DISCUSSION

1. Self-dialogue is open, intelligent dialogue with your own self. It is the exercise that builds a romance with life. Do you live this romance, or have you abandoned yourself?
2. Have you had a roundtable with your fears, anguish, and conflicts? Do you ask: Why? How? Where? What are the fundamentals?
3. Do you have killer windows? Do you lose control of yourself sometimes? Do you react drastically and then regret it?
4. We should use the DCD technique to reedit the unconscious movie and the roundtable of the self to create parallel windows. Do you understand these phenomena? What do you need to reedit in your life? What have you tried to change but were unable to? Hopefully this chapter will encourage you to try again, but with the new understanding you've acquired.
5. Jesus was very concerned with the need for human beings to rescue the leadership of the "self" and fully exercise their free will. Have you chosen your paths, or have you felt incapable of doing so?
6. Do you feel that you have contaminated anyone's memory with your

impulsive attitudes? Are you willing to rewrite your story and attempt to heal the damage you've done?

## Exercises and Reminders for Daily Practice

1. Referencing the characteristics of Principle #6—"Learn the art of self-dialogue"—described in the beginning of this chapter, journal about which ones you need to develop.
2. Talk, debate, and discuss things openly within yourself. Go inside. Become your best friend. Analyze if you have had time for everyone but yourself.
3. Have a roundtable of the self for at least ten minutes twice a week. A good time to use this technique is during your shower: while you wash your body, you clean out the theater of your mind.
4. Have brief self-dialogues a few minutes every day at work, at home, or while you exercise.
5. Turn the tables within yourself. Don't be passive; disagree with your unhealthy emotions. Do not accept any frustration without filtering it first. Question it. Do not accept any conflicting idea without debating it.
6. Don't submit to the control of killer windows. Reedit your unconscious movie and create parallel windows. Practice the roundtable of the self and the DCD technique throughout your life. And remind yourself: freedom is an accomplishment.

## CHAPTER SEVEN

*Principle #7:*

# Contemplate Beauty

When we consider what it means to "contemplate beauty" in life, these twelve statements provide examples:

1. Educate your emotions to turn small things into a wonder and delight for the eyes.
2. Allow everyday moments to become magical experiences.
3. Learn that tears irrigate existence as rain irrigates flowers.
4. Unveil the beautiful, simple, and hidden things around you.
5. Discover the flavor of water, the breeze in your face, the aroma of flowers, the dancing of the leaves in the orchestral wind.
6. See beyond images and hear beyond sounds.
7. Look with the eyes of the heart.
8. Learn to be rich apart from money, to be happy without a reason.
9. Live peacefully in spite of the pressure of responsibilities.
10. Find romance and poetry in life.
11. Embrace your children, admire your elders, and have pleasant conversations with your friends.
12. Allow art, music, and literature to motivate the release of creativity within your mind and soul.

## The Loss of the Contemplation of Beauty

The level of anxiety and tension in modern society is high. Everything moves so fast, even in the lives of children, that people spend little time observing, listening, or contemplating. Children quickly grow bored with their toys, teenagers with their clothes and electronics. The "fast food" mentality is prevalent: drive through, pay, consume, forget. Pleasure has to be sought and paid for rather than discovered or encountered; beauty is overlooked. Contemplation and discovery are not required in order to "succeed."

But a mind that thinks correctly learns to excel at contemplating beauty. This discipline is very important to make our minds more creative, inspired, passionate, and at peace, and to illuminate the parts of our lives that are unseen by the eyes.

I believe much of the ugliness and pain we observe in today's world is the result of human beings losing the ability, even the responsibility, to embrace beauty in all its forms. Did it ever strike you as a "responsibility"—a way to be a caretaker of this gift of life?

Think of the number of people for whom addiction, immorality, violence, depression, anger, and despair are a normal way of life. We have failed to train our senses to be receptors of the beauty that surrounds us. As a result, fewer and fewer people are living beautiful lives that entail grace, creativity, and purpose. I believe even those who think they give credence to the beauty in the world are only scratching the surface of what is there and the impact it can have on their lives.

I have tried to educate my three daughters in this area. I have told them that there is beauty in everything except for human violence, hatred, and destructiveness. "Even in the cracked plaster of an aging wall," I have said. Yet how often do we walk by "cracked walls" without a second look?

When my oldest daughter once asked me, "How can there be beauty in a cracked wall?" I told her to look beyond the physical appearance. "Ask yourself, 'Who made this wall? Why? What were his dreams in building the wall? What did he talk about or think about when he built it? Where is the builder today? How old is he? What would he think if he saw these cracks in his wall?"

None of the answers are on the surface of the wall; they are all beneath. And to see them requires reflection and contemplation; that is, time—the commodity we seem to be most short of today.

Everything has a story to tell if only we will pause long enough to listen.

## Emotional Desensitization

Let me give you a technical term that I use as part of my research: *psycho-adaptation* (psychological adaptation). Other researchers mean something very different with their use of the term, but in my theory and in this book, psycho-adaptation is, in short, the process by which we become desensitized to feeling pleasure or pain when repeatedly exposed to the same stimulus. The automatic registry phenomenon (ARP) imprints the same stimulus on the memory, over and over, until it is nothing new. Therefore it loses privileged status—and the emotions that accompany such status—and we cease to become excited. At that point, it is as if our memory were saying, "You've seen this all before. It's not noteworthy, so don't bother paying attention."

Obviously, this can be an advantage, especially with negative stimuli, but psycho-adaptation affects all aspects of our lives, even what is beautiful. Consider the following examples . . .

## Healthy Psycho-adaptation at Work

Psycho-adaptation[1] drives scientists, sculptors, painters, musicians, dancers, and writers to discover, create, and experiment. When creative types become psychologically adapted to the same stimuli within their environment, it results in an unconscious anxiety that pushes them to seek new stimuli, provoking new levels of creativity. This is an example of positive psycho-adaptation stimulating the mind to be inventive, original, imaginative, and innovative.

If it were not for psycho-adaptation, a boy who loses his mother would be emotionally paralyzed, never recovering from the loss. The mother's death generates continuous painful stimuli. Psycho-adaptation causes the child to adjust to his new situation, decreasing the intensity of feelings that result from his loss. Emotionally, the child makes room for new interests; he adapts to his mother's absence so that his suffering is not so intense. This unconscious process expands the horizons of our minds and emotions.

In every situation of frustration or loss, if a person remains a spectator and the self doesn't direct the thoughts or manage the emotions, then psycho-adaptation will not be sufficient. Thanks to their rich imaginations, children unconsciously and automatically move from the audience to become the director, but as adults we need to give up being passive spectators and become active administrators. If we don't—if we restrict the process of psycho-adaptation—it is possible to develop an insecure, depressed, closed personality.

While writing this book I received word from home that a dear friend had just lost his twenty-year-old son in a car accident. The boy was special: he worked with his father on their family farm; he was kind to others, sensitive, and intelligent. I was told that my friend was completely desperate. Because of the pain of having to answer people's questions, he had already isolated himself from those who were trying to comfort him. He didn't want to talk to anyone.

I called him. The first thing he said was: "Cury, I've lost my life; it has no meaning. I've lost my best friend. I don't want my farm. I don't want to see my boy's pictures. I don't know what I will make of my life."

His words touched my heart deeply. After pausing for a moment, I told him that there are at least two paths to follow in this situation: he can orbit around this loss and become a depressed person who never again makes sense to his wife, his other sons, his friends, or his boss. Consequently, he will lose the thirst for happiness and meaning. Or he can manage his thoughts and scream inside himself, "I will honor my son for each day I lived with him! I will have relationships with people without the fear of talking about my son, because my son will live in my heart. I will look at the pictures and be thankful for each day that I had with him." I told my friend that the feeling of loss will never disappear, but that he needed to resolve the desperation, anguish, self-destruction, and the feeling of "What could I have done?"

After twenty minutes my friend was talking with me about his son, spontaneously and without desperation. "I hear you," he said. "I will honor my son. My suffering is great, but I will look intensely for opportunities to pay tribute to him."

This is the attitude we all need to provoke the formation of healthy psycho-adaptation. Since then I've called my friend a couple of times, and he has thanked me each time. But I don't deserve his gratitude. He has put his remarkable mind to work and chosen to think correctly in this dramatic situation. And because of that choice, he and the family are okay. Even after the violence of their storm at night, their morning has dawned with new light.

## When Psycho-adaption Works Against Us

Psycho-adaptation can have a destructive effect on our emotions too. Nazi soldiers during World War II grew accustomed to the suffering of those who were imprisoned in the concentration camps. They became callous to the horror, feeling nothing at the extreme pain and anguish they were causing. The cries of the children, the malnourished bodies around them, the desperate old men didn't touch their hearts. They lost the ability to empathize, to have compassion for others. As a result, they felt free to inflict even more pain.

Many leaders of governments and business have become psychologically adapted to the frenetic pace of their lives, desensitized to everything except their work. They stop seeing people as individuals and focus only on their ambitions. They often live in palatial homes designed and built by artisans, but they rush past the artwork and craftsmanship without even noticing. They may be financially rich, but their emotional selves are impoverished.

Fame is another arena where psycho-adaptation takes a toll. People become used to the applause and the spotlight, and their emotions develop a need for stronger stimuli in order to experience pleasure. The same is true with drugs—greater doses are necessary to experience the same high. People who find themselves psycho-adapted to stimuli such as fame and drugs find themselves unable to cope in normal society. They can become lonely (even when in a crowd), depressed, or agitated when their source of stimulation is absent.

Especially in our modern societies, the adulation of a select few by the masses is a sign of our illness. Celebrity not only gives the famous a false sense of their value; it creates a depressed sense of value among those who adore them. Don't get me wrong—it's fine to applaud and appreciate the exceptional skills and accomplishments of others. But every person has attributes worthy of being applauded. To make famous only the beautiful, athletic, or wealthy is to make those qualities unnaturally important.

## Rejuvenating Emotions

A correctly thinking mind is ever young, always dreaming and creative. But an ordinary mind loses the pleasure in life over time. If you contemplate beauty, you will always be young in your personality, regardless of what time does to your body. You can employ plastic surgery to try to restore an appearance of youth, but if you do not learn to contemplate beauty, you will grow old emotionally.

Women, here's a particular danger to be wary of: when you complain to your husband about the effects of aging on your body, it can shift your husband's focus from your inner beauty to your outward age. It is much easier for a man to fall out of love with a woman who is obsessed with growing older, for she is no longer secure in her own skin. If aging is what you focus on, your age may well become all he will eventually see. You need to feel and act beautiful more than you need to look beautiful. Indeed, a woman who contemplates her own inner beauty and cultivates it daily will look more beautiful over time than a woman who focuses only on outward beauty.

There are many young women in our culture who are already emotionally old as a result of neglecting their inner attributes (sometimes they look prematurely aged as well). They don't love life, they are dissatisfied, and they are experts at seeing defects in everything. No matter who you are, these are not attractive qualities.

To expand your mind (women as well as men), focus on developing your inner attractiveness and contemplating the beauty that surrounds you. The highest quality of life is hidden within the simplest things. To recognize and benefit from such beauty is a skill that must be developed to have the ultimate life you desire.

## How Our Model of Thinking Correctly Contemplated Beauty

According to the texts of the New Testament, Jesus' life was put in serious danger at a very early age. Before he reached his second birthday, the reigning king in Judea, Herod, sought to have him killed. Jesus' parents, Joseph and Mary, fled with him to Egypt until it was safe to return. So stress was an early part of his life.

He grew up as an apprentice to his father, who was a carpenter. This meant he lived a very physical life, working in the hot sun with tools and rough wood. His was very much a "blue collar" upbringing, not a life of social privilege.

Because he grew up in Nazareth—an area judged to be socially marginal compared to the sophistication of Jerusalem—and because he likely lived at a subsistence level economically, we might have expected Jesus to develop an anxious personality characterized by insecurity, discontentment, and resentment. Yet his words reveal a kindness, gentleness, and peace wholly out of character with such a background.

Perhaps the slow, intricate process of creating an object of beauty or function out of a tree trunk gave him time to contemplate and observe details—life beneath the surface. And that same ability would later be seen in his interactions with individuals.

Just as Jesus saw flaws in the wood he worked with, so he observed flaws in human nature. Yet he valued each person in spite of his or her imperfections. He chose to see beauty instead of weaknesses, potential instead of limitations.

The crowds could sense his empathy for them, and they identified with him far more than with the religious leaders or upper classes of their day. They hung on his words and followed him wherever he went. They saw in him the simplicity and beauty that perhaps they wanted to see in themselves.

But because of his popularity, his simplicity and sincerity would be put to a serious test.

## A Mind Thinking Correctly Extracts Much from Little

Two things often happen to people who experience the kind of rise in public popularity that Jesus experienced: first, they make time for their outward, public world by ignoring their inner, personal world; second, they lose their simplicity and sincerity when they become social stars.

I have noticed a direct correlation in people's lives between an increase in financial and public success and a decrease in personal quality of life. They spend less and less time with the people they profess to love and in activities that give them pleasure. This did not happen to Jesus. He seemed to stay rooted in the soil of consistency. Throughout the three years of his public life, during which time he rose from being an unknown to being the most famous person in Israel, he never changed in his capacity to appreciate the simple things of life. Instead, he allowed these things to nourish his emotions.

On one occasion (what is traditionally known as the Sermon on the

Mount[2]), the crowds were pressing in all around Jesus. He began to teach his disciples truths about the kingdom of God. After many teachings based in the theological traditions of the nation of Israel, he said something totally different: "Look at the birds of the air. . . . See how the lilies of the field grow."[3] No doubt there were birds flying overhead, or perhaps searching for seeds and insects in the grass nearby. And there were likely lilies growing within sight—perhaps he pointed to them as he spoke.

What was he doing? He was appealing to something not found in the texts and legalese of the day. He was appealing to his followers' emotions, to their sense of beauty. He was encouraging them to contemplate something with which they were surrounded every day but which they likely, in their hurried lives, never paused to think about.

What was Jesus' point? It was that the birds had everything they needed to live full, happy lives. And that not even Solomon, Israel's grandest king, had ever been dressed as beautifully as nature had dressed the flowers of the field. He was speaking to people whose lives were consumed daily with the need to provide for themselves. While their lives might have been less complicated in many ways than our modern lives, their anxieties and preoccupations were entirely the same. In their own ways, they rushed about accomplishing the necessities of life just as we do.

Yet Jesus appealed to their emotions by pulling deep truths out of simple and beautiful realities. He was training their minds to think differently, to be sensitive, joyful. He was trying to vaccinate his listeners against the disease of emotional superficiality.

While the people clamored for Jesus to work miracles on their behalf, he sought to open their eyes to an even greater miracle: the beauty that human beings are able to access within themselves and the world around them if only they will open their eyes and the windows of their soul. Jesus wanted them to discover how much truth there was to be found in simple things—seemingly imperceptible things.

As the healthiest individual, psychologically, ever to walk on planet Earth, we would do well to observe how Jesus lived and learn from it. He lived a simple (not simplistic) life, totally aware of the people and events with whom he interacted. He lived "in the moment," as we say today. He wasn't upset about something he'd said the day before or worried about a meeting he was going to have tomorrow. He let life unfold in all its complex beauty and focused on the task and people at hand. He lived deliberately, not impulsively; willingly, not driven by external forces.

By reading the parables (stories) Jesus told and noting how many references he made to the world around him (nature, agronomy, fishing, building, birds, flowers, bread, water, animals, ceremonies—and especially children), we can see how deeply he contemplated life. He used common elements like these to promote the art of thinking in his listeners, stimulating them to make connections in their minds.

The more you and I live that kind of contemplative and exploratory life, the healthier we will be psychologically—the more fully human.

## Following Our Model

It's possible to misinterpret what imitating Jesus' life might mean in today's world. We don't have to live like Francis of Assisi, who gave away his possessions, even his clothes, in order to be unencumbered by material matters. Nor do we have to be like Gandhi or Mother Teresa, or like monks who take vows of poverty.

Learning to contemplate beauty is not as simple as divesting oneself of material goods. Even if we give away all we have in order to clarify our vision of what is most important, the world is full of ten thousand times more than our offerings. Even if we withdraw into a monastery to escape the distractions, there is no escaping the mind. As Jesus himself taught, it is not things outside of man that defile, it is that which springs from the heart and mind.[4]

Therefore, our challenge is to develop the ability to see beyond those things that might fill our vision, whether they belong to us or to the world around us. I've treated some very wealthy people in my country, but I saw much misery living in palaces. They were wonderful individuals, but they had forgotten to cultivate the territory of emotions and appreciate beauty. We must never forget that to achieve a rich mind, we need training to extract much from little things. This training—and practice—must be for our entire lives. This is a spectacular secret of gaining the quality of life you long for. Have you found it?

---

*Thinking Correctly to Contemplate Beauty:*
# Discovering pleasure after nearly half a century of depression

Lucy was an eighty-two-year-old woman who was quick-witted and incisive. She was also pessimistic, ill-humored, aggressive, intolerant, rude, and impulsive. And she was bored nearly to death. Nothing gave her pleasure, not even her children.

Though she hated psychiatrists (she felt that they were charlatans who took the money of others but did not solve their problems), here she was, sitting in front of me. Her daughter-in-law had brought her, skeptical that I could help Lucy, for she had both a superior and an indifferent attitude that made her almost impossible for others to deal with.

The first thing Lucy told me was, "I'm here because I wish to divorce my husband and my family won't accept it. I can no longer live with that man!"

She'd been married for over half a century, I scratched my head and wondered why she hadn't made this decision years ago. Actually, as it turns out, she had spoken of separation countless times, but since her husband was the only person who could stand her, she didn't have the courage to divorce him.

Her husband was about her age. He had been a renowned medical professor. Unlike her, he was calm, reasonable, and tolerant. Yet she was always in conflict with him.

Lucy was an authoritarian, dominating, and excessively critical woman. She said that she had been depressed for nearly fifty years. She'd been a sad teenager too. I believed she might have serotonin deficits, but I could also see that she perpetuated her chronic depression by not protecting her memory. Specifically, she didn't have the ability to filter stressful stimuli. Any opposition would steal her peace, invade her mind, and thereby get registered in her memory by the AMR phenomenon. As a result, her memory became a trash bin of the events that disturbed her on a daily basis—compost for the killer windows and zones of conflict that weren't reedited. What made it worse was the fact that unconscious phenomena that read memory, such as the auto-flow, attached themselves to these windows and produced pessimism, negativity, anxiety, and depressive moods.

Just as she didn't know how to protect her memory and transform it into a garden of wonderful experiences, she also didn't protect the memories of others. (Unhappy people are experts at forming unhappy people.) Every day Lucy would find a reason to cause friction, complain, argue, and express her bad humor to someone. She thought that her enemies were outside of her, and she was great at pointing her finger at others but never critiquing herself. It was as if she were a goddess among commoners. She considered people to be stupid, undeserving of her respect. She was incapable of praising or motivating anyone. (Even her own children were never affirmed.) Everyone was flawed except for her. Everyone had hidden agendas except for her. In her mind, she was the one who was transparent and true.

During Lucy's treatment, I tried to question some of her absolute truths, but she reacted badly. Once, when I encouraged her to question her position in terms of her husband, she was aggressive toward me and got up to leave, threatening to never come back. (Fortunately, she composed herself and sat down.) She was running away from herself, but she wasn't running away from her illness.

She would accept no advice or correction. No one had ever been able to enter her world. I was sitting before one of my greatest challenges as a therapist.

Exploring her psyche was more important to me than exploring an unknown planet, so I needed to change strategies, free my mind, shatter my paradigms. I couldn't criticize her, encourage her self-criticism, and expose her mistakes as everyone else had done. My challenge was to encourage her to open the windows of her memory as much as possible so that she could see me not as an invader of her personality who intended to control her, but as someone who would encourage her to be healthy. I hoped that if she'd only open these windows, she would view her circumstances and her relationship with her husband in a new, balanced, and wise way as well.

Despite Lucy's aggressive reactions toward me, I told myself that I couldn't reject her, not only because I was her psychiatrist and psychotherapist, but also because she was a human being and, as such, had the same value as I. Her mind had magnificent abilities and potential, just like yours and mine do. I reminded myself that Lucy was more important than the theoretical body of ideas that I used to understand her and treat her. I wanted to free her blocked abilities, so I would need to widen the spectrum of my mind to find ways to create strong ties with Lucy.

Helping her through the last phase of her life was crucial. I asked myself, "What is this woman's psychological treasure that no one can see? How can I provoke her mind to have insights with which to react through multiple angles? How can I motivate her to contact her reality so that she can reedit her memory?" I knew that my challenge was to encourage her intellect with the intention of creating parallel windows of beauty to support the construction of healthy thoughts and images.

I began to explore her psyche like a miner searching for diamonds. Since she was very aggressive and self-sufficient, I did not interpret her reactions; I led her to do her own interpretations. I bombarded her with questions and encouraged her to think. At the same time, I exalted her intelligence, affirmed her sharp mind, and demonstrated my admiration at her answers.

She became enchanted with my compliments. First I won her over through the territory of her emotions, and then through her reasoning. Thus, the therapeutic dialogue flowed like a fountain. In the midst of all this, my image was being registered in a privileged way in her memory. In this way, I achieved something that no one else had. During this process of questions, answers, compliments, emotions, and reasoning, countless parallel windows of light were produced in her memory without her knowing it. Her "self" became illuminated so that she could understand her conflicts and correct the paths that her life had taken.

When we produce parallel windows and encourage the self to direct the theater of the mind, a marvelous phenomenon occurs: the effects of antidepressants and tranquilizers are enhanced in the brain's cortex. The therapeutic process itself speeds up as well. In this case, this withdrawn, aggressive, and proud woman opened the doors of her mind and let "air" in; she allowed herself to be invaded by a soft breeze. Our tense sessions became pleasant and productive. I discovered a fascinating person whom no one else knew, perhaps not even Lucy herself. Her aggressiveness gradually gave way to generosity, her arrogance gave way to humility, her fear gave way to security, and her depressive moods gave way to bubbly joy. Each session was a discovery.

We learned a lot from each other. She taught me that each human being possesses a world to be discovered. That no psychic illness is so serious that it cannot at least get better. I learned that it's never too late to develop the most important functions of our mind. I learned that there could be a heroine under the skin of a villain.

Living half a century with a psychological disorder without giving up on life hadn't been easy for Lucy. Perhaps she'd been stronger than any of us, even though everyone had considered her to be fragile.

Her improvement was striking. She gradually began to filter stressful stimuli, protect the delicate territory of her memory, and broaden her horizons. She trained her mind to contemplate beauty and began to enjoy the little things in life. She started to pay attention to people and admire them. She would pause to observe ants, butterflies, and flowers. No one understood how a woman who had been so ill-humored and cranky for decades could now be happy, motivated, and sensitive.

She even began to see her husband through different eyes. She stopped being a torment to him and became his rock. Since she had learned the art of complimenting in therapy, she started to compliment him and love him in a way she'd never done before. Over the years of living with Lucy, his posture had slumped and he had become weakened and pale. But the changes in his wife's behavior surprised him so much that he walked taller, grew more energized, and even started to eat better.

Their love grew so much that Lucy would tell me, to my astonishment, that they had started dancing in their living room like two teenagers. The friction between them gave way to a splendid affection. She would touch her face to his and declare her love for him. She would also take his hands and caress them while she called him "my darling."

That was how Lucy spent the last years of her life with her husband. Touched by her fascinating recovery, I wrote her a short message and asked her to read it together with her husband. It said, "*Congratulations! Both of you have demonstrated that investing in human beings is worthwhile. You have found dignity after the longest of storms. You have transformed the desert of your lives into a beautiful oasis. You have become poets of life.*"

They had the message framed and hung it in their living room. Our minds are so incredible that from youth till our last breath, it is possible to transform an entire life's story. Lucy's transformation reminds us all that investing in a garden of dreams is still worthwhile, even if everyone shakes their heads and says that it's not.

## Suggested Topics for Reflection and Discussion

1. Contemplating beauty means being wealthy without having huge sums of money. Are you emotionally wealthy, or do you lack the bread of joy? To contemplate beauty is to write a poem with your life. Have you done this somehow?

2. Emotions can age quickly. Are you young in the territory of emotions, or do you feel that you are aging, stressed, and assaulted with preoccupations? Are you an ill-tempered person? Do you have psychosomatic symptoms?

3. One of the causes of anxiety, impatience, and dissatisfaction is the

failure to contemplate beauty. Are you a specialist in pointing out your flaws in the mirror? Is patience woven throughout your story?

4. Jesus lived through stress and loss from his childhood on, but he was healthy and tranquil. Pain built him up. He became a craftsman of the human personality because he was a great observer. Are you a great observer? Can you extract pleasure from simple things? Have you set free the child that lives within you?

5. At the height of his fame and commitments, our model of sensitivity did a lot with very little. How about you? Have you done a lot with very little? Are you buried in your activities?

## EXERCISES AND REMINDERS FOR DAILY PRACTICE

1. Referring to the characteristics of Principle #7—"Contemplate beauty"—described at the beginning of this chapter, write in your journal about which ones you need to develop.

2. Make a list of the beautiful things that surround you. Pay attention to the details of a painting, the anatomy of flowers, the style of your house, the behaviors of people.

3. Take care of your plants. Write poems. Refine your pleasure in reading, painting, and singing. Roll around playfully on the rug with your children. Value the things that are simple.

4. Practice feeling beautiful internally as well as externally. Beauty is in the eyes of the beholder. Don't be enslaved by the standard set by the media.

5. Take ten minutes a day to sit in contemplative silence. Or during work, do a little one- to two-minute relaxation exercise and observe the beautiful things around you. Contemplating beauty fuels the pleasure in living. Talking about quality of life without contemplating beauty is like building a mirage.

## CHAPTER EIGHT

*Principle #8:*

# Unleash Creativity

No one has ever discovered the limits of the human mind, and no one ever will—because there are none. And that means there are no limits on human creativity. Here are ten ways to think about what it means to unleash your creativity:

1. Discovering and walking in the paths of your own uniqueness
2. Being willing to live outside the constraints of schedules
3. Learning how to overcome routine and build oases in the desert of tedium
4. Opening the windows of intelligence to make new discoveries
5. Being willing to imagine new possibilities
6. Releasing your emotions and becoming excited about your own possibilities
7. Surprising those around you in a positive way
8. Entering the world of those you love, getting to know their dreams, joys, and fears
9. Learning to live with a mind unencumbered by tradition, expectations, and limitations
10. Turning life into a great adventure

## The Suffocating Routine

The principle of unleashing creativity is complementary to the principle of contemplating beauty (chapter 7) because both require getting in touch with parts of the human psyche that have been considered unnecessary according to the priorities of modern life.

They're a lot like Sunday afternoons. Though an excellent case can be made that the downtime of Sunday afternoons helps your productivity on Monday, many people nowadays would like to do away with Sunday afternoons. Why? Because it is unstructured time (at least apart from football season). As much as we complain about having to go back to work on Monday, we actually look forward to it because it is the routine we know. Our regular weekly routine frees us from the often uncomfortable responsibility of being alone with ourselves and having to decide how to spend our free time.

More and more we live in routines that are suffocating to the human spirit. We follow the same schedules, eat the same food, drive to and from work the same way, follow the same patterns of communication with our spouses and children, and meet our needs with the same solutions. In other words, we do not live life very creatively. When we have downtime, we tend to fill it with the offerings of Hollywood—we would rather fill our minds with the creativity of others than take time to be creative ourselves. But those who learn how to unleash their creativity expand their minds to become more imaginative, inspired, and visionary.

## How Is Your Everyday Life?

There is a difference between material and psychological quality of life. Many a society in this world offers a high quality of life materially speaking, but by and large, the people living in those societies lack existential meaning. Success in one area does not guarantee success in the other.

One reason for our psychological poverty is that people's lives are bound by routines that do not allow for the development and expression of their spiritual and emotional lives—the sources of creativity. It's not uncommon to come across people who work for years at the same place and never surprise their coworkers by doing or saying anything unique or different. They are rigid and formal in terms of how they express themselves. In fact, workplaces are filled with suffocating individuals who would love to shout out what they really think or feel but who don't feel free to do so. They accumulate new information daily, but it's just information. It does nothing to help them become more fulfilled people. Ironically, the challenges companies face in today's global business community require more creative solutions than ever. Yet employers do little to stimulate the very creativity they desperately need.

I could say it this way: An ordinary mind is misused; it rarely breaks from its daily routine to enhance creativity. A correctly thinking mind, however, frequently breaks from its agenda to see life from different perspectives. This can be accomplished in small ways, not just the major ones.

Have you ever considered giving a box of chocolates to the security guard at your company or the superintendent of your building, for example, and telling him that you appreciate him? He will never forget you, because you have surprised him. Whenever we break from our routines, people remember! And when our creativity impacts them in a positive way, it changes their perception of and appreciation for us.

Something as simple as starting a conversation with a stranger in an elevator, instead of staring at the blinking floor numbers, could radically impact that person's day—even his life. We've all heard of people who have ended up getting a dream job or making a lifelong friend or meeting her future spouse, simply because they didn't waste an elevator ride.

Sadly, we are a species that hates loneliness but does everything to perpetuate it. How do we perpetuate it? A good example is the number of children who know nothing of their parents' inner lives—their thoughts, dreams, and concerns. Granted, young children may not be capable of appreciating such intimate knowledge, but teenagers and young adults certainly are. Adults who don't talk to their children teach those children not to talk—and that's what they do when they become parents themselves. The cycle can be broken when someone decides to be creative and do something unusual or unexpected: "Have I ever told you about . . . ?" A simple act of creative expression on our part can open doors to new experiences and relationships, even within our families.

## Consequences

Once there was a father who was deeply disappointed with his son's behavior. The son stayed out all night, went to bed at dawn, didn't respect his father, and showed no remorse for the suffering he was causing. The father would yell, scold, and criticize his son, all to no avail. They were like two enemies who lived in the same house. In desperation, the father decided to change his attitude completely and see what would happen.

He looked for creative alternatives to the methods he was using that obviously weren't working. He opened his mind to thinking in new ways. He began to surprise his son by telling him he loved him and apologizing when he became irritated. He began to praise and value his son. Over time, the young man formed a different image of his father in his unconscious and realized his life could change completely. He became responsible, affectionate, and sociable. The father had courage to break from his routine, and his behavior stimulated the son to be more sensitive and to think before acting.

What brought about the change? That phenomenon called AMR (automatic memory register). As I explained in chapter 4, AMR automatically imprints all images, thoughts, and emotions in our memory. The boy's new images of his father—which included loving and kind words and actions—gradually filled his mind. Because the father's ways were different, they were like surprises; they caught and held the son's attention and eventually attracted his affection.

If parents, teachers, and other adults in positions of influence don't surprise young people with creative ideas and responses, the AMR phenomenon will have nothing to work with. No surprising and positive images will be painted on the canvas of the child's mind. However, when adults open up to children and live transparent and vulnerable lives, kids respond and remember and replicate the creativity.

Telling stories to children is one of the best ways to reach them emotionally—to take advantage of the AMR phenomenon. But in any realm, with people of any age, we choose how we transmit information, and that choice makes a difference. We can deliver the raw data in a monotone, or we can do it via a story or other creative means that impacts our listeners emotionally. Doing the former may touch the intellect, but doing the latter will touch the life.

Employers would be wise to learn this principle. If they never surprise their employees, if they operate their business in the shadow of timeless routines, work gets done, but the employees die a little more every day, and in the long run, the bottom line is affected. The high-tech, dot-com boom in the 1990s saw the rise of many start-up companies that fostered creativity with innovative workplace policies. People were free to experiment, to "color outside the lines"—and good things happened. A fair share of companies today—for example, Google and Yahoo—continue with creative approaches to how they treat their employees. And the waiting list of people applying for employment at these companies extends beyond the horizon. They must be doing something right.

On a personal level, obsessive-compulsive disorder is, in a very general sense, a life devoid of creativity. When one becomes enslaved to routines—excessive neatness, hand washing, eating rituals, lock checking—it is a sign of enslavement. Psychological energy needs an outlet. When that energy is not expressed in creative ways that balance the routines of life, it can only be directed to the routines. (This is a generalization, not a clinical statement on the cause of OCD.)

Social systems, our own choices, or the environments we're in can numb us as much as any drug. When we fail to surprise ourselves and others with creative expressions of life, we become predictable and dull. The consequences of such a lifestyle are a lesser quality of life and many missed opportunities and relationships.

## How Our Model of Thinking Correctly
## Unleashed His Own Creativity

Jesus was a master at using creativity to provoke learning and promote deep reflection on the part of others. Take the instance when Jesus was denied three times by one of his chief disciples, Peter. After Peter denied knowing Jesus for the third time, Jesus "turned and looked straight at Peter."[1] He didn't speak verbally, but he spoke volumes nonverbally by this simple act.

What was Jesus saying to Peter? In spite of his own suffering at that moment, Jesus searched for his disciple's eyes. He knew that Peter was shackled in a prison of fear and shame for having lied three times about his relationship with Jesus. A psychological analysis would reveal that Jesus was probably concerned Peter might be so overcome with guilt that he would attempt to take his own life. But with his eyes Jesus communicated, "I understand you. I love you. I'll never forget you." A correctly thinking mind never fails to be generous and tolerant, even when others disappoint.

Instead of resorting to violence against himself, Peter went outside and "wept bitterly." With each tear came a lesson in life. A simple gaze had communicated more to him about forgiveness and understanding than a thousand words could have. Jesus surprised Peter by his action, and it was the lesson that surprise communicated which stayed with Peter.

No one acted as ingeniously as Jesus. His mind was brilliant, and he was totally unpredictable in what he said and did. As a result, his accusers often found themselves struggling to respond to him because they were not used to anything but stock answers. The lack of creativity and inner depth in his opponents put them in stark contrast to Jesus in the eyes of onlookers. On many occasions, people (including his own disciples) were "amazed" at Jesus' words and the results of his actions.[2] It is no wonder that he is considered to be the greatest teacher in the history of humanity.

Jesus was especially creative in his relationships with people. For instance, instead of shunning lepers, as was the custom of his day, Jesus touched them, ministered to them, and socialized with them.[3] He treated them as normal human beings who had a need he could meet. He used his creativity to communicate to society that they were wrong in how they treated outcasts—but he did it without saying a word.

Jesus lived his life apart from routines and protocols that would have kept him from liberating others. And we should model that approach to life.

## A Model of Sociability

I have never analyzed a human being who was so well resolved—in whom the discordant elements of humanity found their confluence in perfect harmony. Jesus of Nazareth exuded joy. He seemed to love to participate in small celebrations such as weddings and large events such as national religious festivals. He dined in the homes of friends and opponents alike. He was even called a glutton and a drunkard because he liked to socialize so much.[4]

While neither of those two labels was accurate—they were spoken in derision by his opponents—they are telling psychologically: there can be no routine and habit when it comes to interacting with people socially. Think of anyone you know who is the life of the party. You never are sure what to expect when that person is present—he or she is completely open to the moment and responds spontaneously at every opportunity. Inevitably that person ends up drawing other people out—pulls them out of their reserved and inhibited mind-set and involves them in this party called life.

Jesus once met a man on the street named Zacchaeus—a hated tax collector—and invited himself to stay at Zacchaeus's house! Can you imagine? Who would do that? Within a short time, after being in Jesus' presence, Zacchaeus repented of his dishonest ways and completely changed his approach to dealing with people.[5] Jesus' very presence—his surprising desire to want to spend time with Zacchaeus in his home—

was enough to cause Zacchaeus to initiate his own process of internalization and reflection, and eventually to change his behavior.

Simply being with Jesus was an invitation to progress into correct thinking, to develop spontaneity and creativity. He told fascinating stories, answered questions with questions, and left people wanting more. No one ever complained of being bored with the routine when around Jesus. Even his opponents couldn't stay away from him. The question is, How many of our friends and loved ones feel that way about us? They will, if we learn to unleash the creativity that slumbers within us.

Be sociable. Give yourself to others freely and with vulnerability. Surprise yourself so you can surprise others. Make this promise to yourself: From now on I will never again dance the waltz of life with my legs bound. I will free myself in order that I may free others who are similarly bound.

---

*Thinking Correctly to Unleash Creativity:*
# A victim of the dictatorship of beauty

George, a sixteen-year-old, had all the symptoms: a vague, unmotivated look about him; dry skin; a weak appetite. His body was extremely thin, without any muscle tone, and you could see his bones. He was five and a half feet tall and weighed a little over seventy-five pounds. George had developed a disorder called anorexia nervosa.

He never smiled, didn't play any sports, didn't go to parties, and rarely took the initiative when talking to people. He had blocked his creativity and his enthusiasm for life. He was just another victim, among millions, of the most serious dictatorship of modern times, the dictatorship of beauty. Before I tell George's story, I'd like to comment briefly on this subject so that we can better understand his story.

The dictatorship of beauty is caused by the exaggerated value we give to thinness. Though the ultrathin bodies of the magazine and TV models are genetic exceptions to the human species, we treat them as prototypes and patterns of beauty for all. This exaggerated value, expressed in the media, and especially in the fashion world and the sale of cosmetic products and services, is registered by the AMR in a privileged manner in both the conscious and unconscious memory. These windows generate zones of conflict that imprison the "self," dominating its capacity to manage emotions and direct thoughts. Ultimately the person's self-esteem ends up being destroyed on various levels along with his or her self-image (the image one has of oneself both physically and mentally).

The dictatorship of beauty is not in itself the only cause of psychological disorders, but it is, without a doubt, one of the main causes that triggers anorexia nervosa, bulimia (compulsive eating followed by feelings of guilt and forced regurgitation), and overtraining (the compulsive need to exercise excessively to build bigger muscles). By creating an unhealthy pattern of beauty in the collective unconscious, it causes a psychic disaster.

Research says that only 3 percent of women feel beautiful. This number is astonishing. About 1 percent of the world's population develops anorexia nervosa. This seems like a small number until you realize that in the United States alone, there are almost 3 million people suffering with this dramatic disorder. In the world, that number reaches about 50 million—a number greater than the population of many countries, as great as the number of casualties during World War II.

I once went to a high school football game in Tennessee. Both teams had cheerleaders encouraging their teams. All the girls were thin. But how is it possible to have only thin girls as cheerleaders if one-third of the teenagers in the United States are clinically "obese" to some degree? Even in this country that respects human rights so much, this subtle and devastating dictatorship is at work. Just think of the anguish of the overweight girls watching only thin girls performing.

The destruction of self-esteem and self-image inhibits the optimism, creativity, daring, self-confidence, and self-determination of the human mind, making it unhealthy and underused. George was a victim of the tyranny of beauty. Who was controlling his image of himself? The concrete, naked, visible reality, or the distorted picture imprinted in his unconscious? You already know the answer. Every day he would look in the mirror, and despite being down to skin and bones, if we asked him why he didn't eat, he would say, "I'm fat!"

It is simply incredible how we can be a puppet to the images that we create from our killer windows, images that motivate us to react in illogical and self-destructive ways. Gifted executives can feel paranoid. Scientists can suffer from imaginary cancer. Women can believe they are pregnant when they aren't.

George didn't listen to his parents. He wasn't influenced by his friends and teachers either. He only listened to a penetrating voice that emanated from his mind. His parents, an engineer and a teacher, were desperate, for their son had a ritual during meals that enslaved him and disturbed everyone at the table: he'd weigh all of his food on a scale and count his intake of calories.

Every psychic ritual binds our mind and ties down our creative capacity. George ate very little and had no pleasure in eating because he was afraid of gaining weight. He knew that he might die, but he never abandoned his routine. Mealtime was horrible for the entire family.

His parents no longer knew how to react. If they criticized their son's behavior, the already serious situation would get even worse, and George would refuse to eat that meal. The fear that their son would die made his parents hostages of his disorder. The drama was augmented because he refused any treatment with psychologists, pediatricians, or even nutritionists.

It is possible to have a psychological disorder and not be seriously ill; in other words, to recognize that you are troubled but ardently desire to be the protagonist of your own story. But it is also possible to be psychologically ill while having a very ill "self" that is passive and indifferent, that focuses on its illness and doesn't have the great dream of change. These people are harder to treat and are the ones who drag out their disorders. George was in this situation. That's why I always say that the biggest problem is not the "illness" of the "ill" but those who are "ill" because of the "illness."

George's anorexia and subsequent anemia got so bad that he no longer had the strength to walk the three hundred yards from his house to school. His parents cried for their child who had abandoned himself, who seemed to want to give up on life.

Their last resort was to force him to be institutionalized. That was when they came to see me. At our first meeting, after I became acquainted with the facts, I didn't talk much about George's illness; I wanted to get to know the human being who was ill. I knew that George listened to no one and refused any form of guidance. I felt that I could only help him overcome his drama if he were challenged to leave the audience, stop gravitating toward his illness, and become an independent, secure, and free person.

The risk was huge. He could stop treatment at any moment, so it was fundamental that I gain his trust. I couldn't become his hostage like other professionals had. I couldn't treat him with pity, and I also couldn't be harsh and excessively critical. I decided not to behave like a psychotherapist who was above him, but as a human being who was really interested in getting to know his story and explore his interesting world.

I'd have to be creative to stimulate his creativity. I'd need to surprise his expectations and register my image in a positive manner in his conscious and unconscious memory. I wanted my words to echo within him in a way that his parents' tears hadn't. So I began by reviving his dormant dreams and pleasures. After conquering this terrain during the first few sessions, I prepared a foundation in his unconscious to challenge himself, to encourage him to break from his routines and rituals with food and recycle his false beliefs.

George said that he actually felt pleasure in eating and that he knew he might die, but he was afraid to call it to the attention of others. I told him that he was unconsciously using his illness so that everyone would give him attention.

I respectfully showed him that he had become a kind of god to the people around him in that they lived for him, and I commented that he had an extraordinary, powerful, and creative mind but that his behavior was destroying him. I suggested that he needed to rescue his inner leader and stop being the slave of beauty. I showed him how his conscious self was imprisoned by images archived within him and how the destruction of one's self-image occurs.

We discussed the fact that both male and female models are also slaves of the tyranny of beauty. Many of them drastically reject certain areas of their bodies. They are anorexic, bulimic, and depressed far above the average for people their age. And if they gain a few pounds, they are discarded. "If they beg for the bread of self-esteem," I said, "imagine the population in general."

I asked him several times what beauty was, what it meant to be beautiful, what self-esteem was and how he would describe freedom. He concluded that beauty is unique, individual, and belongs to each human being. If beauty really is that free, I challenged, then being dominated by the dictatorship of beauty is prison. I told him that it was his choice whether to be free or a prisoner of a social system that uses extremely thin models to generate dissatisfaction in the majority of people (because a dissatisfied person is more anxious and thereby consumes, or purchases, more). Finally, I told him that if he lived in the Amazon rain forest, isolated from modern society, he'd probably never have anorexia and would never stop listening to the voice of billions of cells that were crying out to live. His "self" truly had to be autonomous if he was to be free.

George was positively surprised with the therapeutic dialogue. He would internalize our conversations and question himself as a traveler who seeks for springs of water. As part of his treatment, I asked his parents to be kind to their son but to stop centering their lives around his illness; they shouldn't overvalue it, because to overvalue it would be reinforcing it. His parents began to treat him not as an extra-special son, or an overly fragile one, but as an important member of their family. They began to talk about other things, focus on new projects, and enjoy more adventures. And his parents' behavior echoed inside of George.

Over the following months, the AMR phenomenon registered

George's new experiences in the landscape of his personality, creating fresh paths from which he could see life and react in a healthier way. He learned how to overcome his torturous routine, and he abandoned his calorie counting and started doing unscheduled things. A young man who'd barely had the energy to walk so expanded the horizons of his mind that he began to dance the waltz of life with freedom and grace.

It wasn't through magic that he overcame, and it took a lot of time. George had several relapses in the beginning, but he understood that conscious and unconscious memory are formed by thousands and thousands of windows, and that some unhealthy windows only manifest in particular situations and environments. He understood that each relapse wasn't reason to blame himself; it was a precious opportunity to reedit windows that contained conflicts that hadn't been worked through.

Years later he sent me a message from dental school, filled with joy, freedom, and motivation. His message ended with these words: "Thank you so much. I am now 150 pounds of happiness."

## SUGGESTED TOPICS FOR REFLECTION AND DISCUSSION

1. Freeing creativity means turning life into a great adventure. It means being open to other possibilities, having pleasure again, making new discoveries, and appreciating challenges. Have you freed your creativity, or are you enclosed within your routine?

2. Surprising others is fundamental to building an excellent image in their unconscious. Do you surprise others? Are you able to enchant them when they make mistakes or frustrate you? Do you say things you've never said before?

3. Obsession is a source of anxiety. Do you have fixed ideas or repetitive behaviors that disturb you?

4. Jesus enchanted people. Everyone had access to him. He knew how to praise, encourage, and motivate people. He had a contagious joy and sociability. Do you feel that you live in a cocoon? Do you feel that you need to open up more?

EXERCISES AND REMINDERS FOR DAILY PRACTICE

1. Referencing the characteristics of Principle #8—"Unleash creativity"—described at the beginning of this chapter, journal about the ones that you need to develop.
2. Surprise yourself. Do things that are healthy and pleasurable.
3. Surprise others. Talk to your children, friends, parents, and coworkers with tenderness and transparency. Ask questions you never asked before. Tell them how important they are to you. Hug them.
4. Greet those who have "simple" jobs in a way that will communicate to them that they are very important.
5. Economize on criticisms and judgments, but spend lavishly on compliments to those you love or work with.
6. Spend a weekend at someplace new. Walk different paths. Drive new routes to work. Give flowers on unexpected occasions.

## CHAPTER NINE

*Principle #9*

# Be Restored in Your Sleep

There is likely no aspect of human well-being so important yet so neglected by modern man, as sleep. Here are the essentials of deep, restorative rest that create an environment for the mind to think correctly:

1. Your sleep restores the physical and psychological energy expended the previous day.
2. You fall asleep quickly and sleep soundly (not waking up excessively).
3. You sleep deeply and pleasantly.
4. You're not tormented by nightmares or exhausting dreams.
5. You don't take problems and conflicts to bed.
6. You wake feeling rested, motivated, and equipped to face stress and challenges.
7. Your sleep keeps you alert and concentrated for a good intellectual performance.
8. Your sleep makes you calm enough to make well-thought-out decisions.

# Counting Sheep

It's no coincidence that the people who shortchange themselves when it comes to sleep are usually the same people who complain about the quality of their lives. Have you ever noticed that? They have no idea that adequate sleep, and the resulting restorative rest, is nonnegotiable. People who don't value their sleep don't love their lives.

A mind that thinks correctly gives great importance to restorative sleep. Sleep is a treasure that not only produces peace but enthusiasm, and that makes us more discerning, competent, and able to think before reacting. It is simply impossible to reach your potential in any area without adequate sleep.

Human beings should spend one-third of their lives asleep. From a purely anatomical perspective, sleep is when the human body does its most important work. Cells relax and rebuild, excretory organs process waste, and the cardiovascular system is given the much-needed opportunity to decelerate. During sleep, thoughts slow down, emotions quiet, and your conscious "self" leaves the complex state of awareness that it's in all day long, taking a break from reading and processing millions of bits of information. The mind enters the unconscious sphere of relaxation during which the level of psychological energy drops significantly. In essence, the body rests for eight hours in order to fight the battle of survival for sixteen hours.

# Sleep and Health: Consuming Cerebral Energy

I am always amazed at conferences when I ask the attendees how many of them wake up feeling tired; how many have a hard time concentrating; how many feel sleepy during the day. There are always a large number of participants who raise their hands. People are literally carrying their bodies around during the day, forcing them to perform in spite of physical, emotional, and mental energy deficits.

These are professional people who are good at what they do but who are not happy with the way they do it day in and day out: fatigued, restless, yawning, daydreaming, falling asleep, and irritable. Due to the stressful lives they lead, these professionals use up lots of cerebral energy each day. They need a minimum of eight hours of restorative sleep—perhaps nine or more—but they try to function on much less than that.

If the minimum amount of sleep is actually insufficient for people who expend large amounts of physical or mental energy in a day's time, think of the cumulative impact of getting too little sleep for months on end. Laboratory experiments have shown the mental aberrations that begin to occur in subjects who are sleep-deprived for longer periods of time. Depressive and anxious crises are usually preceded and perpetuated by insomnia.

Depression often manifests itself along with excessive drowsiness. While drowsiness can be an involuntary mental escape from stressful stimuli, it can also be a desperate attempt by the brain to rest and replace long-depleted stores of energy. When a person seems depressed and experiences uncontrolled outbursts or explosive anger, fear, or irritability, one of the first things to look for is lack of adequate sleep. This is true of children as well as adults. Large numbers of children struggle to make it through the day because they are sleep-deprived and malnourished. (Yes, wealthy, developed, Western nations have untold millions of children who don't get the nutrients their bodies need to provide energy for daily living and physical growth.) Children who stay up late watching television, text-messaging or IMing their friends, or surfing the Internet will in time suffer poor academic performance. There will likely be a drop in their motor skills as well.

The good news is that some methods can aid your body in getting the maximum benefit from the hours you do sleep:

1. Exercise at least three times a week for a minimum of thirty minutes. Physical exercise, besides providing aerobic benefits related to moving oxygen throughout the body and to the brain, liberates endorphins—

natural mood enhancers that promote feelings of well-being—leading to relaxation and sound sleep.

2. Avoid eating before sleeping. Anytime food enters the body, it puts the body in work mode (digestion), not rest mode. It's hard to sleep soundly when your body's digestive furnace is hard at work. Instead, begin relaxing at least a half hour before bed: read a good book, listen to relaxing music, spend time meditating or praying, take a relaxing bath, or enjoy a quiet conversation.

3. Sleep in as dark a room as possible. Melatonin, a hormone produced by the pineal gland in the human brain, aids in promoting sleep. Light (even small amounts) inhibits the release of melatonin, while darkness stimulates it. The natural rhythm of the human body is to sleep during darkness and work during light.

4. If you are an insomniac and cannot sleep for more than two nights, you may need the temporary help of a prescription sleep aid in order to give your body the rest it needs. Do not persist in fighting insomnia and risk becoming sleep-deprived.

5. Do not take your enemies and problems to bed. The New Testament's maxim to "not let the sun go down on your anger"[1] is universally excellent advice. Jesus trained his disciples to resolve the problems of the day in order to devote sufficient time to sleep. There is nothing you can do about your problems while you are sleeping, so if they can't be resolved, they should be set aside so as not to rob you of the rest you need. A person who thinks correctly understands this, but an ordinary mind will not accept it.

6. Learn to view your bed as a refuge, a safe harbor from the storms of life. Sleep should be treasured and protected as a personal sanctuary, a time when you thank your body for its previous sixteen hours of hard work, a time that you reserve for yourself as an investment in the high-quality life you desire. You can train your mind to release the cares and concerns of the world if you will seek to learn this discipline.

7. Even if others don't deserve your forgiveness, forgive them for your sake. Don't let someone who has wronged you once wrong you a

second time by stealing your sleep. Let it go, and let your mind be at peace.

## How Our Model of Thinking Correctly Restored Himself with Sleep

Jesus was at such peace within himself that he could sleep any-where—even in the midst of very stressful situations. He was a carpenter by trade with little experience on water. Yet when he and his disciples were caught in a violent storm on the Sea of Galilee, it was his disciples—some of whom were experienced fishermen—who panicked. Not Jesus. Jesus had lain down in the boat to take a nap and would likely have slept through the entire storm if the disciples hadn't wakened him.[2]

Once awake, Jesus challenged their anxiety and lack of faith. They were insecure, allowing external circumstances to throw them into a state of agitation. They were even frustrated with Jesus because he had been calm enough to take a nap while they were on the verge of being swamped.

Jesus had just made the point to his disciples that he had no bed to call his own[3]—a reflection of his social and economic status. So he learned to tune out the world and sleep wherever he was and whenever he needed rest. And he slept deeply—even in a storm-tossed fishing boat in the middle of an inland sea. His mind was remarkable and determined, as only a properly trained mind can be.

Why was Jesus able to shut out the world and sleep like this? Because he was not preoccupied with the gravity of the problems confronting him. It was not as if he lived a carefree life. He was continually hounded by his religious opponents and lived under threat of death. He shoul-dered the welfare of his disciples and multitudes of other followers as well. But his mind was at peace. When it was time to rest, he did not take his problems to bed. He cared for others' needs, but he didn't worry about their needs. He didn't give up his peace in order to take on their physical, spiritual, mental, or emotional problems. He knew how to protect himself from the mental thieves that would steal his sleep if he allowed them to.

## A Master of Forgiveness

A life of relationships with others is a source of both pleasure and stress. Friends, spouses, children, coworkers, strangers—all can bring immense pleasure or intense pain. Clashes are inevitable in the cauldron of relationships. Not to deal positively and creatively with those clashes is to invite mental and emotional turmoil that can rob you of peace—and of sleep.

Jesus was a master at relationships, managing them so they did not become negative forces in his life.

1. He took immense pleasure in social conviviality.
2. Giving to others irrigated his life with meaning.
3. He expected nothing in return from others.
4. He knew that all people lose their patience and coherence in the throes of tension.
5. He was aware that the strong understand and the weak condemn.
6. He loved people regardless of their mistakes.
7. He calmed his emotions by mastering the art of forgiveness.

While all of the above are worthy of our imitation, the most important principle in terms of this chapter is number 7: mastering the art of forgiveness.

It is a fact that many professional therapists—psychologists and psychiatrists—do not know how to use the tool of forgiveness themselves; nor do they know how to help those they counsel practice the art of forgiveness. I have treated several of these professionals who were caught up in the web of social conflicts and didn't know how to resolve them. In short, they didn't know how to forgive.

A person who thinks correctly knows that the first person to benefit from forgiveness is the one who forgives. Jesus maintained his own peace of mind and heart by forgiving without being asked. He who was sinned against by so many took it upon himself to be the forgiver. He understood the internal miseries of those who were attacking him and forgave for that reason. He had compassion on those who were not equipped spiritually, intellectually, or emotionally to do better. If more professional therapists would learn from the way Jesus forgave, they and their clients would enjoy greater peace.

Not to forgive is to nurture and feed anxiety; to nurture anxiety is to live without peace; to live without peace is to live in turmoil during the day and night. Understanding what makes others attack and be unreasonable is the basis of forgiveness. Love helps, but it takes more—it takes knowledge and understanding. That's why Jesus was able to say, from his place of death on the cross, "Father, forgive them; for they know not what they do."[4]

Jesus forgave his own murderers because he understood all to which they were enslaved—the social and religious prejudices of the day; their own insecurities; their ordinary, passive minds; and their self-centered motivations. Even in the moment of his own death, he was free to forgive. Love, understanding, and forgiveness came together at the hour of his greatest pain and suffering.

What is the greatest revenge against someone who has disappointed you? It is to understand his fragility and extend forgiveness. Forgive him and you will be free of him and will have a tranquil mind. Hate him and he will sleep in your bed and steal your rest.

---

*Thinking Correctly to Be Restored in Your Sleep:*
## The terror within a home

Cristina was a frightened forty-year-old woman. She had long, blonde hair and the look of someone who suffered. Indeed she was suffering—from chronic insomnia. Like many women around the world, she also suffered domestic abuse. Michael, her husband, was an authoritarian businessman who couldn't stand being questioned or criticized. All of his employees were terrified of him. He had a neurotic need for power and he always had to be right.

Someone with these two neurotic needs plays the role of a god rather than acting as a human being, generally depriving others of their freedom, shattering their spontaneity, and causing them insomnia. In other words, they make others ill.

Though Michael sought to dominate family members and employees, ironically he had no control over himself. He was financially wealthy but emotionally poor. He was physically strong but psychologically weak, unaware that strong people promote debate and weak people hate it. He thought that his strength lay in his bank account and his deep voice.

Cristina had been married to Michael for seventeen years. They had three children, two of them teenagers. Michael had humiliated his wife many times. During their honeymoon they'd had an argument and he'd had the gall to point a gun at her. Perplexed, Cristina gave in and silenced her voice but also distanced her heart. She cried inconsolably, realizing she had married a man who only existed in her imagination.

Michael didn't know that a few moments can change a life. He had achieved his wife's submission during that argument but had lost something that money and power cannot buy: love. Throughout their marriage, Cristina was continuously abused in several ways, including physically. But she never sought her rights or got a divorce, although she really desired to separate from him.

Cristina remained silent, like many abused women do. Michael had money, she didn't; he was socially powerful, she was anonymous. She was afraid of taking action, afraid of the future, afraid that she wouldn't be able to survive, afraid of not having the resources to take care of her children. Fear is a villain that always silences voices and denies rights.

All of these concerns, along with the lack of support from other members of her family, blocked the positive areas of her mind. Cristina began to lose her brilliance, her creativity, and her security, and she became depressed and ill-tempered. Almost every day she would have nightmares that her husband was beating her or her children. Her sleep, which should have been a holy place to replenish her energy to start a new day, became a source of torment.

Cristina was unaware that the violence she suffered and that her children witnessed was compromising her intellectual, emotional, and social future. No money in the world could make up for that. Michael was destroying their innocence and spontaneity. He yelled at his family on a daily basis and beat them frequently. Their suffering was so great that sometimes his children wished that their father would die.

Michael's strange behavior floated between extremes. He not only expressed the reactions of a violent psychopath but would sometimes cry like a child who feels inferior to his siblings. This fluctuating behavior produced zones of paradoxical conflict within Cristina. She sometimes hated him, but in other moments, when certain memory windows were opened, she felt pity and compassion for him.

The emotional fluctuation of violent men is another important dynamic that causes women who are abused to continue living with their husbands. Their maternal feelings take over their spousal feelings, and so they stay, despite all logic.

Cristina came to see me without Michael knowing about it. At the beginning of the session she began talking about her insomnia. Moments later, she told me about the anguishing causes of her insomnia. She said that this was the first time that she was opening up about the past seventeen years of intense suffering. Desperate, she cried a lot and could barely talk. She was afraid that Michael might attack her or even me, that he would use his gun. So she would sneak into our sessions.

Cristina needed to overcome two things—her traumas and past conflicts, and her fear—and activate her inner leader. But how would she do this? There were many risks. She didn't have the strength or the will to go to the police.

As our sessions progressed, I told her that her worst enemy wasn't outside of her but within her—her fear and her inner ghosts. She was surprised by this line of thought. She had no idea that if she didn't confront her fear and insecurity first, she would never be free on the outside.

Throughout her treatment she got to know her own self and explored the enormous potential of her mind. Week after week she discovered that she had to stop being the victim of her husband to become the protagonist of her own story. It was her great task, her great challenge as a human being, for if she didn't take action in her internal world, she and her children wouldn't survive psychologically, and perhaps not physically either.

Slowly, this fragile and insecure woman began to leave the chaos behind. Little by little she discovered that she wasn't programmed to live a miserable and dominated life. She gradually understood that her mind had vast areas of capability that she wasn't using. She saw that she wasn't merely a partial person but a complete human being who had courage, power, competence, imagination, and the capacity to change things.

I used antidepressants and sleep inducers during the initial phase of her treatment, but she had taken those before. What helped her the most was learning how to stop being a bystander of her own psychological misery. She began to look at reality in a multi-focal way and found that there was a wonderful world awaiting that she had the right to enjoy. She began to overcome her depression, improve her self-esteem, and face her fears—the inner monsters first, and then her external problems.

As Cristina became more secure, though, I became more insecure. I was afraid that she'd turn the tables at home too soon. I had no idea what the consequences would be for her husband. I had no idea what monsters might appear on the day she declared her independence.

When we suffer a major trauma, it dominates our outlook, our view of life, and our expectations, aborting our capacity to fight for the people and things that we love and suffocating our pleasure in living. But a mind that fights for its rights is truly free.

As time went on, Michael noticed that Cristina was different. She was no longer a fragile woman who cried almost every time he shouted. As she began to confront him, he increased his abuse and threatened to kill anyone who crossed his path. During one of their fights, he raised his hands to beat her, and she said that it would be the last time because she would call the police. He held back for the first time.

A violent man became perplexed. The king began to lose his throne. He didn't know who this woman was; who the true Cristina was. She wasn't timid, tearful, and incapable of making choices and decisions anymore. She now knew what she wanted.

Michael began to follow Cristina, wanting to find out what was happening to her. Although he never raised a finger to hit her again, he sometimes accused her of having a lover and shouted that he would kill them both. When he found out that she had been seeking treatment, he was astonished. He hated me. But he also felt he needed to meet me.

He managed to subtly arrange an appointment at my office. In a way, I knew that I wouldn't be able to avoid meeting him, because if he was violent toward those closest to him, how would he respect the ethic that I could not see him as a patient? As soon as he walked into my office, he revealed his identity. After a few moments of tense dialogue where I tried to explain to him that his wife was depressed and needed care, he took out a gun and threatened me, saying that he'd kill whoever came across his path. He added that he'd even kill my children if he had to. He was treating me the same way he had always treated his wife.

I took a deep breath, knowing that he might shoot at any provocation and that whatever I said next was critical. Wanting to first win over the territory of his emotions so that later I could perhaps win over the territory of his reason, I looked this abusive man straight on and . . . gave him a huge compliment. Then, pursuing the same line of thought, I led him to critically reflect on his behavior in a firm tone: "Why would someone so intelligent need a gun to express his ideas? This weapon argues against you. You know that you have a brilliant mind capable of enchanting and surprising people. Use it!"

At those words the aggressive Michael fell apart. Emotionally disarmed, he put the gun away and began crying like a child. This was the beginning—his entire story was about to be rewritten.

Since I also do family therapy, I agreed, with his wife's consent, to treat him also.

Allow me to reflect a moment on this situation. Because we have not grasped the workings of the mind, we have erred since the beginning of human civilization: we first point out people's mistakes—we show them their failures—before we seek to affirm them. This approach has caused many murders, violent actions, suicides, and wars throughout history, for when we criticize others, we are leading them, at the speed of light, into a conflict zone within the unconscious that wields a great deal of emotional tension. As we've seen, this avalanche of tension obstructs thousands of memory windows, keeping people from accessing information that could guide them toward resolution and peace. I would estimate that more than 90 percent of the correction we receive in life does not generate teaching moments; it is either useless or malicious.

So a correctly thinking mind first compliments others, exalts their value with sincerity, opens the windows of their memory as much as possible, and only then points out a person's foolish attitudes and irrational reactions. If we reverse the order, we block a person's capacity to think, reflect, and make healthy choices.

Some might argue, "That's fake; I can't compliment what I don't see." My response, based on more than thirty years of personal observation and professional research, is that every person has something that can be complimented, either because of his or her actions or because he or she is a human being. A generous mind doesn't control, diminish, or make people feel inferior but encourages their abilities and promotes their capacity to change.

Cristina had the right to separate from her husband, and she became sufficiently strong to do so, but she ultimately decided she didn't want to because Michael insistently asked for a second chance. And she gave him one, for she found that underneath the monstrosity of her husband was a child crying out for help.

When Cristina began to face her fears and past trauma, she solved the cause of her insomnia. Her emotions changed from a tempestuous ocean to a serene pond. And as they did so, her nightmares disappeared. Each new day was no longer a battle but a pleasurable adventure.

## Suggested Topics for Reflection and Discussion

1. Sleeping isn't enough; you must sleep with quality. Sleep is life's litmus test. Has your sleep been restorative? Do you wake up feeling tired?
2. Many people live each day as if they were in a battle. Are you buried under your activities? Do you think excessively?
3. Jesus was able to sleep even during stressful situations because he knew how to protect himself. He forgave through understanding. He helped person after person but didn't live in their pain. He knew how to protect himself. Do you know how to protect yourself? Are you an understanding or an impulsive and unempathetic person?
4. Forgiveness is a wonderful sedative. Who are you unable to forgive? Do you find it hard to forgive yourself? Are you too demanding of yourself?

## Exercises and Reminders for Daily Practice

1. Reflecting on the characteristics of Principle #9—"Be restored in your sleep"—described in the beginning of this chapter, journal about the ones that you need to develop.
2. Write about the people who sometimes affect your sleep—who frustrate and disturb you and who you still haven't been able to forgive. Try to understand them rather than resenting them.
3. Practice not taking your problems to bed. Don't buy into problems that don't belong to you. Don't carry the world on your shoulders. You have limits; don't try to be a superhero. Reap serene sleep after sowing a tranquil day.
4. Get regular physical exercise. Physical exercise liberates endorphins in the brain, which are a natural tranquilizer that relaxes you and induces sleep.
5. Read pleasant books before going to bed. Avoid eating two hours before lying down if you have some kind of sleep disorder. Also avoid turning on the TV or the computer half an hour before going to bed.

## CHAPTER TEN

*Principle #10*

# Live an Enterprising Lifestyle

Passivity is accepting whatever script changes life hands you and having an ordinary mind. Proactivity means taking charge of your life's script and being enterprising—using creativity to work through any scenes that bring loss or frustration. Here is what it looks like to daily live an enterprising lifestyle:

1. Creating opportunities and not waiting for them to appear
2. Dreaming big dreams and setting goals to make your dreams come true
3. Expanding intelligence, embracing sensitivity, and developing courage to realize what you love, admire, and need the most
4. Not being afraid of treading through unknown places, even without a compass
5. Learning how to use failures as the pillars of great victories, losses as the platform for gain, weaknesses as the nourishment for wisdom
6. Believing in life and never giving up on it
7. Knowing how to start over again as many times as necessary
8. Always remembering that destiny isn't inevitable—it is a matter of choice

# No Risk, No Reward

It's one of the "facts of life": no one attains quality of life without taking risks; no company or organization, family or team succeeds without risk. But "risk" doesn't mean luck or "destiny" either. It's not a matter of buying a lottery ticket every week and hoping for the best.

The kind of risk that life rewards is achieved by taking up trustworthy tools like the Think Correctly principles in this book and making them work *for* you. That's why individuals and institutions must be open-minded and enterprising—it's how we continue to discover new paths and horizons, how we learn to profit from mistakes and unforeseen circumstances and to solve problems we've never encountered.

Those who live an enterprising lifestyle expand their minds by building thousands of well-lit windows in their conscious and unconscious memory. They work through loss and frustration in ways that turn pain into energy for shaping the personality. In turn, they become optimistic, confident, disciplined, resolute, and visionary people, with clear goals and fulfilling lives, no matter what life sends their way.

# Living the Labyrinth

A labyrinth is an intricate structure of connected passageways with corners to be explored, mysteries to be conquered, and lessons to be learned—but which can be difficult to find one's way through. Sounds like life, doesn't it? Especially with the unexpected turns and situations that present themselves. Our greatest challenge is to enter these mazes with the expectation of learning from them—and to face the unknowns with courage. Humility is necessary, because there will be many dead ends and course corrections along the way. Worse than erring, however, is neglecting to enter in at all. And therefore boldness is critical.

The most dangerous attitude to have when entering unfamiliar territory is arrogance—thinking you know the way. All of life's labyrinths are different, and they exist at every level: personal, familial, relational, institutional, cultural. Trying to enter a maze as a master rather than as an apprentice will result in a prompt dose of humility (like smacking into a wall). You simply can't hope to navigate the uncertain paths of life by forging ahead blindly. This is another "fact of life." On the other hand, you won't find your way by hiding behind your diplomas or your social or financial status. You have to make your way—step out—but with the humility, openness, and discernment of an enterprising person.

What does discernment have to do with it? An entrepreneur of the spirit refines his or her observational skills to notice small changes, wisely assesses what they might mean, and then takes appropriate, timely action: Don't wait until love dies before trying to resuscitate it; don't wait till your children are ill to try to make them healthy; don't wait until you've been surpassed professionally to try to improve your skills.

An entrepreneur of the spirit also acknowledges that life is a mystery and no one knows what tomorrow will bring—but that doesn't stop him from preparing for winter. He anticipates life's eventual realities and then acts accordingly today.

Don't let yourself become like other people: spending more than you earn and treating your money as if it were inexhaustible. Financial stress is one of the great causes of modern anxiety. Many psychological illnesses, broken relationships, and bankruptcies could have been avoided if those involved had prepared for life's seasons and been quicker to see the problems that were on the horizon. Unfortunately, we are slow to notice changes and slow to react. That's why we need to be enterprising.

However, if we fail in any regard, we shouldn't be ashamed of saying, "I was wrong." If we need help, we shouldn't be afraid of saying, "Teach me." If we take the wrong path, we shouldn't be afraid of starting over. An internal entrepreneur isn't infallible or perfect. He falls, just like anyone else. But the difference is, he gets back up again. He doesn't lament his failures; he is thankful for the opportunity to be in the race. His mind isn't controlled by stubbornness and self-sufficiency but is a sponge that absorbs the experiences of others and vicariously draws lessons from them.

Such a person knows the difference between an ordinary leader and a great one. An ordinary leader sees the big mistakes in his or her life while a great leader sees the small mistakes. An ordinary leader watches his house crumble beyond repair while a great leader notices the hairline cracks and prevents the house's destruction.

## Flexibility and Creativity

There are times when our work progresses well, those close to us love us, our friends are near, and our goals are achieved. We find an abundance—a huge "inventory"—of everything we love. Then there are times when demands rain down, boredom surfaces, friends become distant, and discouragement takes over. We feel as if we can't breathe, as though something has sucked all the oxygen out of the room.

At times like these we must choose between venturing into life's labyrinth to regain what we have lost or passively lamenting the situation in which we find ourselves. We must choose between creating the changes we desire or sitting down and waiting for a miracle. We must decide between controlling our destiny or being controlled by destiny.

When standing at the entrance of a labyrinth, it's natural to wonder, *Isn't this dangerous? Won't I suffer even more by going into unknown places? Isn't it easier to stand still instead of changing my attitude to achieve what I love the most? Is it worth taking risks to be a better parent, a more compassionate friend, a more competent employee, a more sensitive lover?* But don't let those questions throw you. Enterprising minds, like business entrepreneurs, will always have doubts. But the prospect of losing what they have, or what they desire, is more painful than the possibility of temporary setbacks along the way. "Enterprisers," my term for those who live an enterprising lifestyle, know that gaining what is desired will not be easy but will be worth the risks in the end. They also know that those who succumb to the heat of their doubts and insecurities will be defeated. That's guaranteed! So why not take a chance?

Here's the difference:

- An enterprising teacher not only teaches his classes with skill but wins over the territory of his students' emotions. He tells them stories, tells them the adventures that scientists experienced en route to their discoveries, and inspires his students' intelligence while preparing them for life.
- An enterprising executive not only works well with the pieces of a venture, such as the hard data and the logistics, but with the people involved—transmitting sensitivity, praising those she leads, casting a vision for the future, staying calm amid the chaos, and demonstrating that difficulties are only opportunities waiting to be found.
- An enterprising lover does not get lulled into thinking that love cannot die. Instead, she cultivates and irrigates the relationship. She enchants her spouse. She frees herself from the prison of jealousy and gives freedom to her loved one. She doesn't waste foolish energy with fights and accusations, for she is aware that life is as brief as dew drops in the heat of the sun. She enjoys their time together as a couple, turning their relationship into a poem, a garden of respect and love.

Unfortunately, not all people exercise their minds in this area. Some husbands only discover that their wives have been deeply hurt when they file for divorce. Some people only invest in quality of life when they are lying in a hospital bed.

A person with an ordinary mind sits around waiting for the things that he needs to happen. A person with a correctly thinking mind goes ahead and cultivates the life he wants day by day. If you learn how to open the windows of your mind, expand the art of thinking, and practice the principles that you are learning in this book, then the labyrinths you walk through won't be dangerous deserts or prisons. Instead, they will be places where you can achieve your most beautiful dreams.

# Ten Keys to an Enterprising Lifestyle

After years of observing enterprisers, and those who lack the enterprising lifestyle, I've compiled a list of the traits I see in those who are willing to navigate life's labyrinths. Enterprisers . . .

1. Anticipate change—they would rather prevent mistakes than have to correct them later.
2. Have acute powers of observation—they can see small cracks in the foundation before others can.
3. Are not afraid of risk—they know that rewards are usually impossible without risk.
4. Don't complain, blame others, lament lost opportunities, or blame themselves.
5. Will change their minds and approach as many times as necessary.
6. Recognize that the route from Point A to Point B is never a straight line—they embrace the mysteries.
7. Never give up on those they love.
8. Love themselves—therefore, they never give up on themselves.
9. Work to control their fate by constructing opportunities for success.
10. View life as an exciting adventure—and are grateful for the opportunity to be alive.

While working as a psychiatrist and psychotherapist and researching the secrets of the human mind, I've developed a foundational conviction: Every human being—king or subject, intellectual or illiterate, rich or poor—goes through difficult times. Even when troubles don't find us, we tend to find them. Being involved in relationships of any sort will ensure that problems arise. But that doesn't make life unlivable; it makes it inspirational. The deeper in the rock the gold is buried, the purer and more precious it will be.

Instead of thinking that people are complicated, think of yourself as the one who will win them over. Instead of viewing your work as stressful, view yourself as the one who can transform it into an oasis. Instead of perceiving pain as a problem, perceive yourself as a student in the world's most precious academy. This is how enterprisers live and work—and ultimately succeed.

## How Our Model of Thinking Correctly Lived an Enterprising Lifestyle

Jesus of Nazareth was birthed in a stable, didn't go to college, was a carpenter by trade, never traveled more than three hundred miles from where he was born, didn't have a marketing team or a military, and didn't control people. In spite of that limited résumé (by modern standards), he became the greatest entrepreneur in history.

He personally invited a small group of young men to follow him. His choices were unusual, for their own qualifications were as unremarkable as his. They were tense, irritable, impulsive, insecure, sectarian, selfish, and individualistic young men when he met them. I doubt if any of them would pass a modern psychological evaluation to work as a manager of people except for Judas—who was apparently more moderate in temperament. But this did not matter to Jesus since he was a sculptor of human personality, a great administrator of people, and a visionary leader. He knew how to turn dreams into reality. His mind was so clear and complete in its thinking that he knew how to create his own destiny and how to help others do the same.

Jesus' disciples caused him a lot of problems, embarrassment, and disappointments. But he wasn't concerned about immediate results. Figuratively speaking, he didn't cut the trees and burn them to get warm immediately. Instead, he waited for the seeds to be ready and planted them to ensure a supply for the future.

He planted the seeds of tolerance, forgiveness, serenity, and love in the hearts of these young men. Then one day he died in the most inhumane way possible. It seemed that his dream was over. But the seeds germinated in his followers' spirits, grew in the heat of their difficulties, and were irrigated by their tears. Finally, these men were transformed into excellent thinkers with a deep concern for others.

The result was that Jesus ended up with a huge forest. Nowadays, more than two billion people, belonging to innumerable religious groups, follow him. And the part of humanity that doesn't follow him admires him deeply. Many of his ideas are found in Buddhism and exalted in prose and verse in the Koran.

History would not be split into two epochs for just anybody either. Only the death of the greatest enterpriser of all could inspire that. Not only did Jesus divide history; he divided the thoughts and hearts of human beings. He won humanity over to his law of love. He did all of this without winning an election, taking up a sword, or spilling a drop of blood.

## Having Nothing, Having Everything

Jesus worked each principle of thinking correctly into the lives of his disciples like a craftsman. It was an excellent learning process that took only a few years. The disciples learned how to be the authors of their story, turn small things into unprecedented beauty, free their creativity, lead their thoughts, govern their emotions, protect their memory, dialogue with others, and dialogue with themselves.

After Jesus' death and departure, his disciples had no money, fame, or protection, but they had what every human being wants: joy, inner peace, security, drive, and a meaningful life. They had nothing, but they had everything. They were discriminated against, but they had countless friends. They suffered losses, but they had hope. They were imprisoned, but they sang happily. Their minds were free.

Jesus didn't promise them a crop without storms, paths without risks, journeys without accidents, or work without difficulties. But he did promise strength in moments of loss, wisdom in moments of torment, and consolation in moments of despair. It was almost incredible, but on the lips of his disciples there was an everyday gratitude for the wonder of life.

They demanded nothing from others and dominated no one. They were promoters of inner freedom. They were tolerant toward their opponents, comforting toward those who suffered, and understanding toward the madness of those who persecuted them. They weren't cultured, but they created a fabulous culture. The letters written by Peter and John reveal a creativity, brainpower, and sensitivity that astonish modern science. The seeds and dream that Jesus planted embrace the most beautiful aspirations of philosophy, psychology, sociology, and the educational sciences—and their fruit is still seen today.

## What Kind of Story Are We Writing?

We are living flames that sparkle for a few years in the theater of life and then are extinguished as mysteriously as we were lit. Nothing is as fantastic as life, but neither is anything as ephemeral and fleeting. We are here today, and tomorrow we are but a page in history. One day we will fall into the loneliness of a grave, and there will no longer be applause, money, or material things. What story will we have written? What seeds will we have planted?

If life is so brief, shouldn't we seek the most beautiful dreams and the richest aspirations in this brief story of time? What is worth living for? What dreams control you? What are your goals and your greatest achievements?

Some people have depression, anxiety, and stress, not because of their childhood conflicts but because of their existential anguish—the lack of a meaningful life. Remember what we have studied: Some have fortunes but beg the bread of joy; they have culture, but they lack the bread of tranquillity; they have fame but are companions of loneliness. Somehow, they missed the target. In all their getting, they failed to think correctly and get understanding. One of the most popular singers in my native Brazil once said that he had everything a person could want except for pleasure in living. Loneliness, boredom, lack of meaning in life, and internal emptiness were not part of Jesus' vocabulary.

Even while Jesus' body was dying on the cross—a time when the territory of emotion tends to rule—he was still a conqueror. He surprised people with unforgettable statements. The Roman soldier in charge of carrying out Pilate's death sentence was won over by Jesus at the foot of the cross. Each of Jesus' reactions was a blow to the soldier's insensibility. Each of Jesus' responses opened the windows of the centurion's mind. Allow me to give you an example of these reactions.

During the most dramatic hour of his crucifixion—the first hour—Jesus suffered unbearable pain. From a human perspective one would expect him to have instinctive reactions to pain. But to everyone's surprise Jesus forgot about himself and cried out to his Father to forgive those who were putting him to death. From a psychiatric point of view, it is impossible for anyone being crucified to have any lucid thoughts; it is even less possible to be affectionate and altruistic.

He said that his persecutors didn't know what they were doing—his way of saying that they were slaves of the system, that they followed orders without reflecting, and that they weren't free. So, with his body in distress, he forgave them without having been asked for forgiveness.[1] He understood incomprehensible men. He forgave unforgivable men. What intellect is this that awes sociology and psychology to this day?

Jesus is one of the most famous—if not the most famous—human beings in history. He is a man who changed history itself, yet he is much lesser known in the magnificent areas of his mind and within the sciences. This is a grave oversight. My goal through the Multi-Focal project is to make him better known in areas where he hasn't been studied—as an excellent educator, psychotherapist, sociotherapist, thinker, pacifist, orator, dream salesman, maker of friends, executive, enterpriser, and promoter of quality of life.

## Following Our Model

When it comes to developing an enterprising lifestyle, there are a couple of challenges involving personal, intellectual, and psychological development. First, some people are more temperamentally suited to enterprise than others. Some love change and pushing the envelope; others like security and the status quo. Some are proactive goal-setters; some are more passive, more compliant. You probably know which of those categories you fit in. If you are not enterprising by nature, you'll need to dial up that aspect of your temperament.

The second challenge relates to everyone regardless of temperament. There is a world of difference between being enterprising in the world of business and being that way with one's own inner psyche. Some people don't want to be "entrepreneurs of the soul" because of what they fear they may find. They don't want to look under rocks and in long-closed closets—out of sight is out of mind. But it's the very tendency to keep things "out of mind" that is hurting us. For all the reasons you've read so far in this book, we need to become students and explorers of the mind—and becoming enterprisers within is an excellent place to start.

---

*Thinking Correctly to Live an Enterprising Lifestyle:*
# The man who was fired for being a good professional

Lucas suffered from accelerated thought syndrome. He couldn't quiet his thoughts, he was forgetful, his concentration was low, and his motivation was depleted. He was always complaining to his wife that he was stressed and had headaches, and that his hair was falling out. Yet in spite of all of this, he was a good employee. He was responsible, he never missed a day of work, he never caused any problems with his coworkers, and he did exactly what was asked of him. No one had any complaint about him.

Even so, he was afraid of being fired. He felt that the company where he worked was a dangerous maze for him; he had to tread carefully. Therefore, he made a point of not contradicting anyone or giving opinions that clashed with his superiors' thinking. He never used his supply of psychological energy to contribute to the solution of the company's problems; he expended it on his insecurities and worries. And one day he received the thing he feared the most: a pink slip.

He was deeply shocked. He couldn't believe what was happening to him. Anguished, he went to the human resources manager and asked why he had been fired.

It was the first time he'd had the nerve to criticize the company's decision. He made his case—"I never miss work; I always do the duties that are asked of me; I never fail to execute the orders of my superiors—and therefore I feel it is unfair that I am being fired. If I'm a good employee, what is the reason for my dismissal?"

The manager's answer perplexed him, "We are firing you exactly because you *are* a good employee."

"What do you mean?" he asked.

"In these competitive times, we don't need good professionals; we need excellent professionals."

"But what's the difference?" Lucas asked.

The answer echoed in his mind like a torpedo. "I'll give you five differences," said the manager.

"A good professional does everything that is asked of him while an excellent professional does more than is asked.

"A good professional corrects mistakes while an excellent professional prevents them.

"A good professional performs his tasks while an excellent professional thinks for the company.

"A good professional follows orders while an excellent professional creatively seeks solutions before the problems are pointed out to him.

"And a good professional thinks about his paycheck at the end of the month while an excellent professional thinks about his future."

This was a new perspective for Lucas. He had never considered that a good employee uses the ordinary areas of his mind while an excellent employee uses the extravagant areas of his mind. He mistakenly thought that those who use the greatest areas of their minds were the great executives. He didn't understand that anyone could develop them.

While he was confident that he was a good common laborer, he was miles away from being a professional who was always in search of excellence.

His only motivation was his paycheck. He definitely wasn't committed to the future of his company; he had no idea where it was headed, if it was encountering problems, or if it was at the peak of its success.

His company needed extraordinary professionals not because it was demanding, but simply because it needed to survive in a highly competitive market that is constantly undergoing change. It was necessary for employees to think big, to think as team members, to think as leaders and not as mere employees, executive or not. The new times required new leadership—leadership specialized in preventing rather than solving mistakes. Leadership that anticipated problems instead of just reacting to them when they appeared. Lucas hadn't understood that working relationships in the modern business world should no longer be vertical, where the boss or executive watches, commands, and dominates his professionals from the top down. Modern relationships should be horizontal, where everyone learns to be a leader within the space he or she occupies; everyone learns how to debate ideas and find solutions.

As a good professional, Lucas had lived in the small world of his duties. It was a false security. He'd preferred silence to taking the risk of expressing his ideas. He'd preferred alienating himself to making decisions. He'd never asked his coworkers what he could do to contribute to their work. He'd never asked his superiors what he could do besides what they requested of him. Lucas had hated it when anyone gave an opinion about his performance. He was unaware that an extraordinary professional charms and motivates people around him, while a common professional goes unnoticed.

The interesting thing about Lucas was that he was the most educated of all his coworkers, yet he was never promoted. He had both college and postgraduate degrees and was well-read but didn't understand people management, couldn't stand pressure, and didn't know how to live outside of his routine. He was a technophobe, afraid of new techniques or technology, but he had never tried to cure this.

On the day that he was fired, he arrived home desperate and inconsolable. He had cold sweats, his tachycardia increased, and his thoughts became even more accelerated. He felt like putting a pillow over his head and never getting out from under it. He was ashamed and couldn't look his wife or children in the eye. For a time he felt angry toward his company and his superiors.

Soon after his dismissal, his wife gave him another shock. She told him, "Lucas, those who look down only see a small world the size of their steps, but those who look toward the horizon see an enormous world to be traveled. Unfortunately, I have married a man who sees such a small world, and I'm tired of it!"

He hadn't expected this from his wife. She had taken his complaining about life, work, and kids with enormous patience. The problem really must be with him! So he spent a whole day reflecting—putting himself in the place of others and trying to see how they saw him. As Lucas got in touch with his reality, he realized that he was a boring, irritating, obnoxious, and inflexible person.

After this prolonged self-criticism, he had a wonderful insight. Instead of lying in bed thinking he was a victim of a predatory market, he decided to go for it. He needed to rethink the way he related to people and the way he viewed the world and work. Lucas opened his mind to consider other possibilities, to see the events of life from different angles. He knew that if he didn't recycle this experience, he wouldn't get another job, and if he did but wasn't a creative contributor, he wouldn't stay for long.

He decided to give himself the most important gift in the pursuit of change: a chance. He began by training himself, on a daily basis, not to be inert, passive, inflexible, or complaining. He sent his résumé to several companies. He went to job interviews with renewed passion and boldness, thus demonstrating the characteristics of an excellent employee.

He was humble but determined. He'd say things like, "I don't know how to do this, but I have an enormous will to learn. If you give me an opportunity, you will be surprised." So he began to captivate people and create opportunities instead of waiting for them to happen. He gradually lost his fear of traveling through unknown places, for he learned how to use loss as a platform for better gains.

His insecurity was still there, but Lucas trained constantly to overcome it. He now debated ideas, gave opinions, found pleasure in challenges, and left his comfort zone. It took months of constant learning. He reedited innumerable areas of conflict in his subconscious and built hundreds of parallel windows that nourished his new attitude toward life.

Failure had been bitter, but it had helped him to unbind his mind; it had worked as an excellent medicine. He had learned not to be passive or quiet, not to work only for his monthly paycheck. He was now committed to people and to the future of his company. He now looked toward the horizon rather than to the sphere of his difficulties.

Lucas learned that only those who use their minds can change their minds. He realized that fate isn't inevitable; it is a matter of choice.

## SUGGESTED TOPICS FOR REFLECTION AND DISCUSSION

1. To think correctly means creating opportunities. Have you created opportunities to achieve great accomplishments? Do you face your labyrinths with courage, or are you afraid of the unknown?
2. Are you aware of the small problems at work and in your relationships with your children and spouse, or do you discover them only when your world is crumbling?  Do you have the courage to once more win over what you love the most?
3. Have you been an enterprising professional, parent, youth, or lover? Have you had the courage to fall and get up again? Have you freed your creativity to enchant people, solve what no one else has solved, prevent and correct mistakes? Have you made a difference in your world?
4. Jesus won people over without controlling, pressuring, or dominating them. Do you expose or impose your ideas? Do you have a positive influence in your world?
5. Jesus didn't promise his disciples paths without risks, journeys without accidents, or work without hardships. But he did promise strength in moments of loss, wisdom in moments of torment, and consolation

in moments of despair. Do you have strength, wisdom, and consolation in these situations?

## EXERCISES AND REMINDERS FOR DAILY PRACTICE

1. Referencing the characteristics of Principle #10—"Live an enterprising lifestyle"—described in the beginning of this chapter, journal about the ones that you need to develop.

2. Among the ten keys to being an enterpriser, choose and reflect on the one you need to work on the most.

3. Don't be afraid of failure, but do be afraid of not trying. Don't join the mass of frustrated people; be prepared for social and professional challenges.

4. Life is a maze through many seasons, with many twists and turns. Therefore, plan your life. Never spend more than you earn, and don't spend everything. No one knows what valleys they will have to cross in the future.

5. If you are an employee, free yourself from the prison of insecurity, and leave the comfort zone of your diplomas and former successes. Be a conqueror. Explore the unknown.

6. If you are a student, value your studies. Love your school and your teachers. Have courage. Be enterprising without being afraid of failing. If you fail, rethink your life, but don't retreat. Think correctly.

## CHAPTER ELEVEN

*Principle #11:*

# Think Existentially

*Existentialism* as a philosophy has a negative connotation—it views life as being unexplainable and man as being a lonely individual who is isolated in an indifferent universe. The word *existential*, however, is an adjective, the core meaning of which is "relating to, or dealing with existence," according to the American Heritage Dictionary. Since we all "exist," we all live *existential* lives, meaning we must all come to grips with who and where we are in the grand scheme of things.

When one uses existential thinking to assess and develop a high quality of life, it will mean

1. being aware that life is a big question in search of a big answer;
2. seeking the meaning of life and an intelligent reason to live;
3. trying to understand, regardless of one's religion and according to one's culture, the mysteries of life and the secrets of the Author of existence;
4. investigating answers for the questions that cannot be answered by science: Who are we? Where are we going? Is the end the beginning or is the beginning the end?

5. being aware of the temporality of existence;
6. finding hope in desolation, comfort in tribulation, courage in loss, and wisdom in chaos.

## Life Is Indeed Beautiful

Because life is very beautiful and very brief, it should be lived with intensity and wisdom—that is, with correct existential thinking and awareness. Thinking existentially makes your mind more serene and wiser, securer and humbler, more imaginative and inspired—even in the face of all that we do not know. So we have worthwhile reasons to explore this chapter.

During all periods of time and in all civilizations, the innate human desire to understand our origins and destiny and to obtain meaning has motivated people to look for an Author of existence in many forms. Man has always sensed that he is an existential being, and therefore religion is the only structure that has never passed away. Nothing—not even the most materialistic of modern inventions, enticements, or movements—has been able to quench the human spirit, the spiritual side of man.

When such spirituality is infused with serenity, it results in social peace and justice, encourages love, and enriches pleasure. But when it is controlled by radicalism and authoritarianism, it produces strife and hatred while suppressing the flowering of the human spirit.

Regardless of how one integrates existential thinking, the same timeless questions persist, among them our wonderings about creation (How did I get here?) and death (What happens when I leave?). The human life is a story with a glorious beginning and an "unacceptable" ending. It is hard enough for us to acknowledge the reality of death, but even when we do, we have a difficult time accepting the idea of the termination of existence, a final nothingness, an extermination of personality. Death only becomes acceptable when it is seen as a chapter in the ongoing story of life.

Man's struggle to define his existence permeates every field of human activity—especially his desire to prepare for, and ideally stave off, death. Whether in law enforcement, the military, medicine, sanitation and health, water treatment and food safety, toxic waste and the environment, or transportation safety—all endeavors are tied to ensuring not only a quality of life for people but guarding against the premature end of life.

Art, literature, and film deal frequently with the end of existence in one way or another. The search for meaning and a connection to God is not normally portrayed as a sign of weakness but a sign of man's intelligence—that which makes him unique among the animal species. Even those who argue for atheism are doing so as a way of providing relief to their existential disquiet. Atheism is their answer to the questions of their origin, purpose, and destiny.

## The Frustration of Science—the Implosion of Atheism

Raising questions about the existence of God becomes more and more timely as science expands. With every passing decade science makes greater advancements. Since the age of the Enlightenment, and then the Industrial Revolution, science seems to have made more advances in every decade than in all previous decades combined. The doubling of human knowledge used to be measured in centuries—now it is measured in blocks of five to ten years.

The beginning of the twentieth century saw a fresh optimism sweep across the globe. Science was supposed to solve all of mankind's most pressing problems, both physical (food, health, quality of life) and social (justice, equality, human rights). It was thought that the twentieth century would be the age in which mankind would finally ascend the throne of supremacy and self-sufficiency, using the tools of science. For the first time in history, man would ask and answer all of life's most difficult questions.

But science didn't deliver. The main thing science did was provide more efficient and horrendous ways for mankind to destroy itself. World

War I ("the War to End All Wars") killed or injured more than nine million people, providing a serious reality check that maybe the twentieth century wasn't going to usher in utopia on planet Earth. In retrospect, it seems that in spite of marvelous technological advances in the latter decades of the century especially, the measures of quality of life have continued to scale downward. Science has advanced, but mankind has regressed. Loneliness, stress, anxiety, psychosomatic illness, ATS, relationship crises, drug dependence— not to mention continual wars and the threat of new diseases and natural disasters—are all signs that man's existential questions have not been and are not being answered by science alone.

As a result, we are seeing the implosion of atheism. It is collapsing under the weight of its own intellectual vacuity, its inability to provide answers to mankind's crisis of meaning. Religion and spirituality, on the other hand, are increasing as man seeks ultimate and practical answers to his growing angst. The Intelligent Design movement is simultaneously gaining more and more support, too, as learned scientists, recognizing the legitimacy of science yet its inability to answer man's deepest questions, seek to integrate the life of the mind and the life of the spirit.

Life is proving to be "transrational"—where we must acknowledge the rationality of science and its benefits but also admit that much of life is beyond rationality and demands a "nonmathematic" explanation. Scientists in the field of quantum physics are conceiving theories that acknowledge that the universe allows for the existence of a "cosmic consciousness," a "divine designer," or a "descending causality." If psychologists would study psychological phenomena and the workings of the mind in as much detail as quantum physicists are studying the universe, they, too, would be conceiving of new reasons to think seriously about the existence of a greater being.

## The Rationale for Eternality

I am convinced that the majority of people who have claimed atheism through the ages have done so because of the insanities practiced by followers of human religion: discrimination, segregation, injustice, the restriction of freedoms, intolerance, wars, and massacres. I also believe that many of those self-declared atheists were, in reality, antireligion and not atheists. I've studied the ideas of leading atheists, such as Diderot, Marx, Sartre, Freud, and Nietzsche, and none of them answered the great philosophical theories that I will put forward here.

One of the biggest questions confronting us all is: Who would place us in the amphitheater of existence to savor life and then, after a few moments, make us say farewell to it? Is it pure happenstance? The phenomena that appeared from the existential void? "Nothing"? Or was it the existence of a higher being—regardless of the name that is given him or the religion that is used to understand him?

Years ago, seeking to abandon the superficiality of my atheism, I seriously studied the possibility of God not existing. I tried very hard to eliminate not just God as a possible author of existence, but to disprove the existence of God himself. After innumerable analyses and intellectual paths, I was perplexed. The conclusion I came to is that it is impossible that God does not exist.

Let me explain.

One can use any theory to explain the universe and nature, from the Big Bang to biological evolution, but none of them can legitimately include "nothingness" or an "existential void" at the beginning of all beginnings.

Can it be philosophically concluded that before there were galaxies, planets, and stars there was an existential void? No!

Is it possible that before the existence of microorganisms, cosmic dust, molecules, atoms, and atomic particles there was "nothing"? No!

How come? Because nothingness would never awaken from the eternal sleep of inexistence for the incomprehensible struggle of existence. The existential void would never abandon its "not being" status to assume the "being" status. Simply put, it's far easier not to exist than to exist. It takes no energy at all not to exist. That's simple science.

So at some moment during the chain of events, a being that has no principle of existence, that has always existed, and that is self-existing has to appear, because nothingness and existential void are eternally inert and barren. Only existence can generate existence. Such an approach sustains a great philosophical thesis: God is not a hypothesis of faith but a scientific truth. If we eliminate a self-existing being from the interminable chain of events, we eliminate the fundamental principle of existence and we return to a complete vacuum, to the tyrannical status of "nothingness."

The human mind develops a meaningful existence and searches for the transcendent either in the continuation of existence after the chaos of death (some form of eternal or ongoing life) or because it cannot sustain the idea of nothingness in the psychological theater. Thus, we should consider all atheistic theses as a form of religiosity that tries to fill the emptiness of nothingness. All forms of explanation are an homage to existence, a conscious and unconscious form of escaping the existential void.

I am not talking about religion here; this book respects any form of belief, including atheism. What I am arguing is that the appearance of existential intelligence is practically inevitable. Therefore I defend that it must be irrigated with wisdom, tolerance, and respect for differences; otherwise, radicalism will surface in various forms, causing mass destruction, as has always occurred throughout history and into our current era. Those who are individualistic, egocentric, controlling, and moralistic have created a god in the image of their psychic unhappiness and haven't developed a brilliant mind that is passionate for existence and embraces life.

## God: Reality or an Invention of the Brain?

Besides the philosophical thesis, there is a psychological thesis that demonstrates that God is not a delirium of the human mind. As the author of the Multi-Focal Psychology theory, I discovered that the greatest evidence for a mysterious transcendental being is not in the physical world but within the core of the human psyche. There were times when I, as a scientifically oriented thinker, rejected the very idea of the existence of God; to me, this was an excursion in the realm of the imaginary and fanciful. I felt that God was the fruit of the brain's imagination, evidence of a mind that didn't accept its limitations, especially its end. But the more I researched the process of thought construction—the final frontier of science—the more my mind changed.

In my research I found clear evidence of several psychological phenomena that exceed the limits of logic. For one, the brain is incapable of explaining its own workings—processes such as psycho-adaptation and auto-flow. Since the psychic energy of the brain is a continuous and unstoppable process, thinking is not an option for human beings—it is literally unavoidable. We can learn to manage thoughts, but we cannot stop them. Such phenomena could only have been initiated by a mysterious Author.

Here's an illustration of another phenomenon at work. Two scientists observing the same data may produce different interpretations because of differences in their skill, intellect, background, powers of observation, and personality. But a single scientist may also view the exact same data on two different occasions and arrive at two different interpretations—without a conscious intent to change. Why does the difference occur? Because we are never the same. The process of interpretation is not linear, mathematical, or completely logical. At any moment in time there may be dozens of variables that produce different chains of thoughts and different understandings.

Another example: a woman doesn't view the same outfit the same way each time she wears it. Each time she puts it on she brings a new psycho-awareness to it based on a multitude of variables. The clothes are the same each time, but she is not.

Likewise, our view of the world is continually changing and evolving even though we are often unaware of the process. Humans have the ability to define the logical system of math where 2 + 2 always equals 4. But they cannot apply that same logic to how they view even inanimate objects such as clothes, art, a car, much less other people or any human experience. One moment we are at peace, the next moment we are anxious. Thus the mind is not bound by the same rules and logic as the worlds of math and science.

"Metabolism" is simply not a sufficient explanation for the brain's creative and totally unpredictable emotional energy or its distorted and complex chains of thoughts. Darwin's theory of evolution, based on mutation and genetic variability, can explain the adaptation of the species in the face of environmental turmoil and flux, but it can't explain the illogical processes that occur in the backstage of the human soul. His theory is too simplistic to unravel what generates the world of ideas and emotions. There is an energy field that cohabitates, coexists, and co-interferes intimately with the brain, but that surpasses its limits. Something that cries for life to continue even when pleasure in living is lost. Something that cries for hope even if the world tumbles over us. Something we call soul, psyche, or human spirit.

The psyche or human soul needs God-existence to explain it.

There is much more to be said on this subject, but I will conclude by stating that the phenomena that build intelligence have convinced me that God is not an invention of an evolved brain that resists its own existential ending (death). I am not defending any religion, but in my opinion God is not an idea of the brain; the brain is an idea of God's.

## Searching for Eternity: the Creative Intuition

If the human mind were strictly logical, the intellectual world would be programmed and rigid. We wouldn't have inspiration, creativity, or doubt. We wouldn't have the vital anxiety that stimulates us to open the windows of the mind to solve it. There would be no authors of fiction nor readers of fiction. So the mind that thinks correctly recognizes and embraces existential thinking as part of its wealth.

The great physicist Albert Einstein developed a mind that thought existentially. Though he once said that he didn't understand where the inspiration for the discovery of his theory of relativity came from, when later asked if he believed in God, he replied that a scientist such as himself could not disbelieve in God. On another occasion he said that he was more interested in knowing the mind of God than the phenomena of physics.

The father of psychoanalysis, Sigmund Freud, sought to overcome the dilemma of existential angst as an atheistic Jew. But love trumped his logical brain. His intense love for one of his grandchildren who was slowly dying of tuberculosis shook Freud's foundations, sending him into a depressive crisis. Was his depression a sign of fragility? Not at all. It represented a dramatic unconscious reaction in the face of death. Freud's depression was an expression of his existential intelligence. It represented a cry from his unconscious for eternity.

I understand what Freud went through. I experienced a similar loss when my sister-in-law and her two sons died in a fiery car crash. My dear brother's wife and sons were family to me, and I would have given anything I possessed to bring them back to life. We cried uncontrollable tears over our loss but did not cry out in despair. What our brains were not able to reconcile, our souls were. Only God was adequate in that moment to console me and my family.

## Psychiatry, Psychology, and Faith

Who are we? Where are we going? How is it possible to rescue the personality's identity after death if trillions of our memory's secrets crumble in the grave? There is an existential conflict like this within each human being—whether you're devoutly religious or skeptically atheistic. No thinker has ever found such answers. Those who searched for them within science died with their questions.

Thus neither psychiatry nor psychology can fill existential emptiness or provide answers to the mysteries of life. Psychiatry treats psychological disorders by using antidepressants and tranquilizers, and psychology treats them by using psychotherapeutic techniques. They treat the symptoms of the conflict, but they cannot solve it, for at the core of the human spirit is a "black hole," an existential hole that "engulfs" our peace in the face of the pain of life and death. The ending of existence is the most anguishing phenomenon for humans. All cultures have developed some kind of existential intelligence to try to understand and overcome it. But when faith begins, science is mute. Faith transcends logic.

Correct thinking is silent before the faith of people, defending the right of all people right to be respected in their beliefs and culture. Each person should follow his or her own conscience, make his or her choices, and be responsible for them.

## The Personality Characteristics That Can Block Existential Thinking

I believe that living existentially, regardless of your creed, can and should make an important contribution to your quality of life. Unfortunately, being existentially aware and thinking correctly about life's greatest questions doesn't always have this outcome. We can very easily create a god in our own image and use him to terrify and control people.

When it comes to meaning-of-life matters especially, an undeveloped "self" encounters serious challenges. It is more likely to anchor the process of memory-reading in the zones of conflict in the unconscious, thereby promoting self-abandonment. In other words, the self doesn't learn to lead; therefore the individual is more prone to develop a series of neurotic needs that affect psychological health and relationships and that stunt the development of important areas of his or her mind.

What are neurotic needs? They're reactions, attitudes, or behaviors that are reproduced with a certain frequency and compromise the "self" as the manager of the psyche. When they surface, a person's serenity, emotional health, intellectual harmony, creativity, self-esteem, respect for differences, and respect for human rights are jeopardized.

I have identified more than forty of these unhealthy needs. In my opinion each and every human being, to a smaller or greater degree, has a few of them, myself included. I will briefly comment on a sampling of them.

## Neurotic Need to Fixate on Preoccupations

People who struggle with this problem possess a "self" that specializes in brooding. Despite the fact that they might be enchanting people, they live day to day without enchantment. They don't enjoy their achievements; they brood over their losses. They don't exalt what they do have; they are experts in pointing out what they lack and in seeing only difficulties instead of opportunities. They don't enjoy the pleasures of the present because they are disturbed by the possible storms of tomorrow. The future is not a source of adventurous challenge for them but a source of uncertainty.

## Neurotic Need to Be the Center of Attention

Those who have this neurotic need possess a histrionic "self" that likes to take over the social spotlight and get people's attention. They can't stand going unnoticed. They are unable to find greatness in the anonymous things or beauty in the simple things.

Their emotions are bubbly and excessive, but they lack intuitive depth, fulfilling life-projects, and clear goals. They are talkative, dramatic, and exaggerated in a constant attempt to capture the admiration of others. They seem to be concerned with themselves, but deep down they pay a high price to be recognized socially, because they don't know how to filter stressful stimuli. They have no psychological defenses, and their minds are easily invaded by the garbage from outside.

## Neurotic Need for Power

Those who have this need have a controlling, dominating, and authoritarian "self" that is strong externally but fragile internally. When they occupy a position of power, their unconscious monsters appear and produce aggressive behaviors.

They believe that power becomes more important than life itself. They repress the freedom of others and don't respect boundaries. They feel threatened by intelligent people and are afraid of competition, for the fear of losing their power asphyxiates them. In certain cases, they live with the paranoia that there's always someone trying to bring them down.

Throughout history people in the most diverse professions and political offices have tried to eliminate people who think correctly because they felt threatened. It still happens today. Instead of using their power to promote debates, these neurotic authoritarians use it to silence voices. They are gods who don't respect the pain or potential of others. They silence their children, their spouses, their friends, and even themselves because they lose the spontaneity of life. In reality, the more power they have, the less they are.

## Neurotic Need to Always Be Right

Those who have the neurotic need to be perfect cause a psychic riot wherever they go. They have not only lost their humanity; they have difficulty getting in touch with their reality; they don't recognize their flaws, much less admit their mistakes.

Such people are terrible at apologizing but great at defending themselves. They aren't always aggressive in their tone or words, but they are aggressive in the way they act. To defend their behaviors, they ignore or put down the arguments of their children, spouses, students, and coworkers, leaving a path of pain in their wake. And when they do defend themselves verbally, they use every excuse imaginable, even the most illogical and childish, to demonstrate that their ideas and attitudes are correct. They don't understand that it is very comforting to recognize one's imperfection. The neurotic compulsion to always be right produces stress and eventually becomes intolerable.

# Finding Serenity

To expand our existential intelligence and counteract such neurotic behaviors, we need to provide an environment in which to develop the most important functions of our mind:

1. *Expose* rather than *impose* ideas. After you expose your ideas, you should allow others to reject or accept them.
2. Think before reacting. This forces instincts to be examined and checks aggressiveness, hatred, and anger.
3. Have tolerance and compassion. Tolerance is the art of respecting differences, and compassion is the art of contributing to others' well-being.
4. Have love for life and for human beings. Existential intelligence should contribute to the enrichment of human emotion and the development of sensitivity, the capacity to forgive, greater understanding, and wider inclusion.
5. Seek wisdom in the face of stress. This should expand one's capacity for recognizing mistakes, perceiving one's limitations, and understanding the broad aspects of existence.

## How Our Model of Thinking Correctly Thought Existentially

Isn't it interesting that all the millions of scientific books in the world can't explain the two most important phenomena of existence: life and death? Yet Jesus addressed both broad aspects of existential thinking—such as forgiveness, fraternity, compassion, tolerance, serenity, inclusion, and the capacity to work through physical and emotional pain—and fundamental existential conflicts such as the anguish of the end of existence, overcoming death, the meaning of eternity, inextinguishable peace, and final justice.

His words on the transcendence of death and the dream of eternity to this day shake the foundations of medicine, for medicine has no power once we close our eyes on existence. Certainly medicine aspires to prolong life and relieve pain. Philosophically speaking, this is also an aspiration of religion. But medicine is a natural science and spirituality is a transcendental search. We in the medical and therapeutic professions can do a lot for a person who is alive, but we can do nothing for a person who has exited life.

Jesus spoke of both realms—life and death—and how to be equipped for them, because he knew that we live within a universe of mysteries and secrets. But one thing is certain: Someday you will experience the greatest phenomenon since your birth. Someday we will all leave this life without our friends, children, achievements, or social status.

Confucius, Socrates, Plato, Alexander the Great, Napoleon, Hitler, Stalin—none of them escaped death. In the end, they eventually bid farewell to the brief stage of existence, just like we all do. Jesus did not flinch at this fact. Yet he also knew no one's life and end would be explained by classical science. That is why he urged people to think beyond the here and now and consider more than just the physical realm.

## Living with What's to Come

Nothing has as drastic an effect on memory and the world of ideas as death. The brain's cortex decomposes, completely disorganizing the patchwork quilt that weaves our story. Without a story, the memory isn't read; without the reading of memory, no chains of thoughts are constructed; without chains of thoughts, there is no existential consciousness; and without existential consciousness, everything and nothing become the same thing.

Because of my research into the process of the construction of thoughts, I am aware of the dramatic consequences of the end of life and cannot view life or the end of existence superficially. People who say they are undisturbed by death are the most fragile emotionally. They talk about something they haven't reflected on. They are the most unprepared for the most turbulent of all existential experiences.

On the other hand, people who have panic attacks over a sudden fear of dying have, from a philosophical point of view, a deeper understanding of human frailty. Their problem is that they lose the leadership of "self"—they don't direct their emotions or manage their thoughts concerning their fictitious image of death. That's why they become ill.

Jesus was fully aware of the anguish human beings feel when facing the end of life. He eloquently defended the continuity of existence and the overcoming of existential conflicts. He wanted each human being to be eternally healthy, tranquil, happy, and wise. He wanted to dry the tears of children who had lost their parents and ease the despair of their tireless search to be reunited with them. He wanted to relieve the anguish of parents who had buried their children—who wouldn't feel their little one's warmth or hear their voice again. He wanted to console those who mourned loved ones, refreshing them with hope. In his teachings on existence and his conversations with the grieving, he relieved fears and produced inner consolation in a way that psychology and psychiatry cannot do.

## The Highest Plateaus of Thinking Correctly

Jesus is unique in that he talked about eternity with passion yet never pressured people to follow his views. This aspect of his existential intelligence amazes any honest intellectual who analyzes him. It would be easy to assume that when he helped people, it was for the purpose of enticing them to follow him. After all, that's how we humans operate! But he didn't use his apparent charisma and power to make people gravitate to him. On occasion he even told the people he'd helped not to tell others about what he had done. He had no interest in attracting a following built upon miracles or signs and wonders. His maturity and gentleness are almost incomprehensible.

His ethics were like a fragrant aroma in the stale religious air of his day. Unlike most of us, what he did with one hand, he didn't tell with the other. Any politician or leader nowadays loves to proclaim his or her feats for the sake of media attention. But Jesus, the model of quality of life, asked that his accomplishments be kept quietly beneath the public radar.

He became an unprecedented social phenomenon. In spite of his own efforts, it was impossible for someone with his intellect, attitudes, and teachings to remain hidden. But he preferred to be discreet. He once told a parable that encouraged discretion and humility, the very virtues he himself practiced. The message of the parable was this: When you are invited to a banquet, you should take the least obvious seat, the place with the least social visibility. If you take one of the most prominent seats, you might end up being embarrassed if the host asks you to move to make room for a dignitary. But if you sit in the least prominent seat, then you might be honored if the host asks you to move and take a higher seat. Better to be honored than humiliated, Jesus taught.[1]

This parable applied to his life in that he did not spend his time seeking a place of honor in society. He simply did what he came to do in a humble way, leaving others to make their own evaluations of his words and works. He did not hesitate to associate with people who might not be good for his reputation; he associated with those who had needs he could meet, regardless of their social status. The only time he accepted being elevated above others was when he was raised upon a Roman cross to die.

Science, through its foolish pride, has ignored the wisdom of the Master of masters, ignored the thirst for existential intelligence that is the essence of every human being. Fortunately, the intellectual winds are changing. Human beings are completely free to be atheistic and follow their own conscience. But there is no doubt that the development of existential thinking through prayer, meditation, and the search for meaningful answers not only resolves inner conflicts, quiets thoughts, and calms the waters of emotion, but makes the psyche healthy.

## Final Words: An Inexplicable Love

Although Jesus loved being discreet, people were so captivated by him that they couldn't help but follow him. Crowds that included women and children followed him even through deserted places. He exuded a love that attracted the human spirit.

He once preached using a figure of speech that shook his listeners. He said that those who ate his flesh and drank his blood would have eternal life. He was referring to eating from his words and drinking from the fountain of his well-being. But because they didn't understand his intention, some perplexed listeners abandoned him. In this delicate situation Jesus gave his closest disciples the freedom to leave also.[2]

The eternal life about which Jesus preached enters the realm of faith and therefore is outside the sphere of this book. Science is silent in the face of faith. Therefore, those who wish to discuss and understand this subject should seek out spiritual leaders and theologians. What I want to analyze here is the psychological dimension of his behavior and teachings.

Despite the strength of his discourse—proclaiming that he held the secrets of immortality—he had the courage to give his disciples the choice of forgetting about him. He asked them directly if they wished to abandon him or not. The disciples had been with him for two years and did not expect this question. So Peter came forward and said, "Lord, to whom shall we go? You have the words of eternal life."[3] Peter's spontaneous attitude of freely following Jesus is the noblest exercise of the right to decide. The religious and political spheres are where people are most easily controlled, induced, and dominated. But Jesus gave us beautiful lessons in freedom.

He fully lived one of the highest functions of intellect: the art of exposing and not imposing his ideas. He exposed his thoughts without fear or pressure. He let people decide to love him or not—a freedom that even the most sensitive of parents don't give their children unconditionally. For all of us, day in and day out, we directly or indirectly demand a response from people. We want their gratitude, their appreciation for what we do. We give expecting something in return.

To follow Jesus, people had to be free. They had to exercise the famous and very little-understood psychological phenomenon of free will. Let's recall a few facts: Jesus predicted that his disciples would abandon him when he was arrested. But instead of calling them dogs or wolves, he viewed them as docile sheep, confused without their shepherd. He even called Judas his friend and gazed at Peter when he denied him. To both Judas and Peter he was saying, "I understand you!" And he didn't stop at that. He had the sensitivity to forgive those who mocked him and drove nails into his hands and feet during his crucifixion.

Who is this man who loved humanity unconditionally? Who is this man who respected human decisions without argument? Who is this teacher who preferred to always understand and never condemn; who preferred to forget his own cries to dry the tears of others?

He reached the peak of psychological health at the height of human misery. His gestures have no historical precedence. He fully practiced the humanity that philosophers, Buddhists, Muslims, Christian leaders, psychologists, intellectuals, psychiatrists, sociologists, academics, and legal minds have dreamed of. If we lived a small percentage of what he lived, prisons would become museums, police officers would become poets, generals would become painters, psychiatrists would become writers, and airport security officers would become musicians.

All of my experience as a psychiatrist and scientist seems foolish in the face of the dimensions of his love, patience, and wisdom—the fruit of his remarkable existential thinking. I have researched the psychic phenomena that construct the complex art of thinking and the development of intelligence, and it has expanded my horizons, but analyzing the secrets of Jesus' personality has made me aware of my own smallness. The only thing I can do in light of such greatness is become a humble apprentice, a small scholar in his school of thinkers, a simple student in his university of life. And I believe all who examine his life closely will find themselves in the same place.

---

*Thinking Correctly to Think Existentially:*
## The world Einstein didn't know

Existential intelligence is one of the most complex areas of the human mind and one of the most important for psychic and social health. Developing it, as we've seen, means expanding compassion, respect for human rights, and respect for those who think differently. Developing it means learning not to diminish, control, or label others. Just the opposite, it is learning to take in, embrace, give credit to, and invest in each human being even when he or she frustrates us.

In chapter 11 I am giving the last story in applying the principles of thinking correctly, because in chapter 12 my deepest desire is that the principle of "turning life into a celebration" becomes your story. My dream is that each of you will gradually expand the extraordinary, beautiful, and surprising areas of your minds and will in turn celebrate your existence.

In this chapter, the application of the principle "Think Existentially" will be excerpted from a book I wrote called *The Future of Humanity*. Despite the fact that it's fiction, this excerpt contains a real episode in Einstein's story and a psychiatric debate that deeply touches my emotions.

We've seen that he was a scientific giant and developed his existential intelligence, but he failed in a fundamental area—and with someone he shouldn't have failed. Relatively few people know of this side of Einstein, however.

In the fictionalized discussion you're about to read, fundamental matters linked to existential intelligence are argued, such as labels, prejudice, and the discrimination that patients with psychic disorders suffer. What must remain at the forefront is that each human being, regardless of his or her psychic disorder, has the same dignity and deserves the same respect as the most illustrious of intellectuals. We can help them not only with affection, support, encouragement, techniques, and medication, but we can also learn from them.

Every human being has a lot to learn and a lot to teach. Those contaminated with pride are the worst students in the school of existence.

———

*The main character of the book is a young psychiatrist named Marco Polo who, like his namesake, is also a traveler, but a traveler in the world of ideas. In this journey he fights to humanize society, and especially psychiatry, through an intelligent exchange of ideas with his professor.*

One day Marco Polo was participating in a meeting to discuss cases. The meeting consisted of ten psychiatrists, which included a few professors and five students. Dr. Alexander, a psychiatrist of great reputation and a renowned professor, led the discussion and concluded the meeting by saying, "Those who do not learn how to diagnose will be terrible psychiatrists."

After the applause ended, Marco Polo replied, "Diagnoses might be useful for me as a professional, but is it ethical to categorically tell our patients?"

"Yes, our patients have the right to know the truth," replied Dr. Alexander.

"I agree that patients should know the truth," said Polo, "but what is this truth that we construct in psychiatry? Isn't it true that our theories are subject to change over the years?"

"Are you questioning psychiatry?" the professor asked impatiently.

"Certain areas must be questioned," Polo replied. "I'd like you to answer me this: should we place our patients within a theory or a theory within our patients?"

The professor thought about this but had no answer. He had written many scientific articles but had never considered this.

Marco tried to simplify his question. "If the theories are above human beings—if they are irrefutable—then we must place our patients within them and label them according to what is presumed. However, if human beings are above the theories and their personalities are so distinct from one another, we should be careful with our diagnoses. The same diagnosis that might serve to direct my conduct might also serve to control a patient and to cause anguish in his or her life."

Marco's other colleagues felt disarmed. Dr. Alexander was shaken with the young man's argument and boldness. He had never faced a situation such as this one, so he tried to avoid the issue: "The fact that patients might suffer because of their diagnosis is a myth."

Marco countered, "There are thousands of people who, living under the dictatorship of labels, affirm that they are depressive, schizophrenic, or bipolar."

Dr. Alexander was feeling vexed. "Don't you think that you are awfully young to be criticizing psychiatry?"

"Professor Alexander, if I lose my capacity to criticize, I'll become a servant of the theories and not a servant of humanity."

Marco Polo saw differences between communicating a diagnosis to a patient with a physical illness and openly diagnosing a patient with a psychological illness. When a patient knows he has suffered a heart attack or has cancer, he can collaborate with the doctors' recommended treatment to perhaps overcome the disease and thus improve and expand his quality of life. Therefore Marco Polo added, "Cancer or heart attack patients are rarely discriminated against because they suffer such illnesses. On the contrary, they frequently receive affection and support, and are visited by friends and family. On the other hand, patients who suffer from bipolar depression or schizophrenia are rejected by family members and excluded socially and are rarely visited by friends. Labels in psychiatry generate a cruel and unjust isolation."

"I don't label my patients," said another professor.

"I'm sorry, but sometimes we label them without wanting to," said Polo. "The manner we use to give them our diagnoses can generate an emotional disaster. They lose their identity as human beings and interject the fact that they are ill." Marco took a breath and added, "And what about the power of labels? Einstein once said that it is easier to disintegrate an atom than a prejudice."

The professors were intrigued by the young doctor's poise and boldness. Philip, who was also a resident, said, "Einstein was a genius. If he said that, we must be careful. We might cause more harm than help to patients."

Marco concluded, "Einstein himself suffered prejudice on two occasions."

"When?" another psychiatrist asked.

"The first time he was a victim of prejudice, and the second time he was the agent. The first time occurred when Einstein demonstrated that time and space are interchangeable and belong to the same structure. However, the time-space structure as a whole does not vary—it isn't relative—therefore Einstein himself wanted to change the name of the 'theory of relativity' to the 'theory of invariance.' But he was not allowed to. Why?" he asked looking at Dr. Alexander.

"Because the word 'relativity' had already become popular," answered the professor.

"Correct! The greatest theory in physics was perpetuated with the wrong name. Prejudice had won."

Marco Polo became silent. He had a very serious story to share about Einstein, one perhaps never before heard by anyone in the group, but he didn't tell them what the second prejudice was. He waited until their curiosity produced enough healthy stress in the room that those present would be capable of opening their minds to possibility.

Anxiously, one of the psychiatrists couldn't wait any longer and asked, "What was the second situation?"

Marco declared, "One of the greatest geniuses in history had a mentally ill son. His son was schizophrenic."

Everyone looked at each other in surprise.

Marco Polo continued, "There's a great lesson here. Except for genetic causes, a question comes to mind: if one of humanity's greatest minds had a mentally ill child, who is free of developing mental illness? This question induces us to an anguished answer: no one is free of this possibility.

"But it needs to be rebutted with another question: Einstein was the exponent of logical science, of the physical world and of mathematics; but to have psychologically healthy children we must be exponents in another world—the illogical world of existential intelligence. It involves the emotions, the sensitivity, the flexibility, the dialogue, and the capacity to put ourselves in the place of others and realize their feelings."

The scientists were intrigued by Marco Polo's reasoning and assessed it against their personal stories. It would be expected that psychiatrists or psychologists rarely had mentally unhealthy children. But they also knew that several mental health professionals, including some of the psychiatrists in their group, had stressed, depressed, phobic, timid children who also had other conflicts. All their logical knowledge about the human mind hadn't been enough to guarantee success in forming their children's personalities.

To educate is to till illogical soil. Every human being, including psychiatrists and psychologists, has difficulty walking this treacherous terrain.

Another psychiatrist asked, "What was Einstein's reaction to having a psychotic son?"

"It couldn't have been worse!" said Marco. "This time Einstein wasn't the victim but the agent of prejudice."

"How so?"

"Einstein visited his son at the psychiatric hospital only once," Marco told the group. "He abandoned him and allowed loneliness to be his companion. And in a human being, rejection and loneliness, my dear friends, are as penetrating as the light studied by physicists."

The group was silent. After a few moments of deep reflection, Dr. Alexander himself asked, "Within the limitations of interpretation, what were the causes that you detected that made Einstein abandon his son, since we exhaustively recommend that families not abandon their patients here in this hospital? Why was one of the most brilliant minds in history so blind in this situation?"

Marco Polo took a deep breath and said, "In my humble opinion, there were four causes of Einstein's prejudiced attitude, and they were incompatible with his intelligence. First was the emotional blow he received when he saw the inhumane conditions of the hospital where his son had been committed. To this day our hospitals are depressive. Second was the lack of hope that his son would overcome his psychosis. Third was the dramatic anguish that his son's hallucinations and delirium caused him. Fourth was the fear of having to face his own impotence in an unknown world."

"Einstein's mind was avid for answers, but he must've been disturbed by the lack of answers to explain the fragmentation of his son's intelligence," Dr. Alexander remarked.

After a brief pause to catch his breath, Marco Polo said, "These four causes reveal that the man who best understood the forces of the physical universe hadn't understood the psychological forces, which are the most complex in the universe. Einstein was a gentle man who loved peace, but prejudice had incarcerated him. His 'self,' in this area, was imprisoned by the killer windows or zones of conflict archived in his unconscious. His fascinating story reveals that it is indeed easier to deal with the atom and immense space than with psychological afflictions."

He then concluded by saying, "Gentlemen, each mind is a universe to be explored. Welcome to the most complex area of science!"

## SUGGESTED TOPICS FOR REFLECTION AND DISCUSSION

1. The same existential disquietude that primitive tribes have had, modern man also has. What are we? Who are we? Where are we going? Analyze if these questions occupy the stage of your mind.
2. The human being is a question in search of an answer. Do you realize that life is very beautiful and brief? Does the brevity of existence encourage you to find a deeper meaning for your life?
3. Science has made spectacular leaps, but it hasn't eliminated the physical and especially the psychological miseries of the human being. Do social violence, terrorism, hunger, chemical dependency—in other words, the problems of humanity—bother you? Do you try to help your fellow man in any way?
4. Existential thinking quiets the thoughts, tranquilizes the emotions, and brings consolation in loss, courage in injustice, and hope in chaos. Have you calmed the waters of emotion? Is the future a dream or a nightmare for you?
5. Does the end of existence haunt you? Does the fact that death is an unavoidable phenomenon disturb you? Have you suffered the loss of someone dear, and does it still hurt you?
6. Jesus invited but didn't pressure people to follow him. He exposed rather than imposed his ideas. He surprised everyone with his kindness. He fully lived out the most important features of a correctly thinking mind. Have you lived out the principles we've covered in this book? Has searching for God, regardless of a specific religion, enriched your emotions and your social relationships?

## EXERCISES AND REMINDERS FOR DAILY PRACTICE

1. Referencing the characteristics of Principle #11—"Think existentially"—described in the beginning of this chapter, journal about which ones you need to develop.
2. Explain in your journal what you think of life. Mention your doubts, unrest, and fears about the end of existence.
3. Try to be faithful to your conscience in your search for God. Exercise your free will. Be free. Those who are not faithful to their conscience can never repay that debt to themselves. They are not honest with themselves, and therefore they can't find tranquillity.
4. Rescue your understanding of the meaning of life. Search for something beyond your work commitments and social activities that can quench your spirit and give you motivation to live.
5. Participate in philanthropic activities. Give to your fellow man.
6. Think with freedom and intelligence. Practice exposing rather than imposing your ideas.
7. Evaluate if the practice of existential thinking, regardless of religion, is developing the most important functions of your mind.

## CHAPTER TWELVE

*Principle #12*

# Turn Life into a Celebration

The quality of life that thinking correctly can deliver may seem like a beautiful but unattainable ideal. Yet I am convinced it is attainable. It is just somewhere other than where we look.

Since the dawn of humanity, human beings have sought wisdom—expressed by an amazing mind full of happiness, meaning, health, and creativity—like the parched earth begs for water. Is it easily accomplished? No. Poets have paid it homage, novelists have described it, philosophers have contemplated it, but most of them have only greeted it from afar.

Kings have tried to conquer wisdom, but wisdom did not submit to their power. The wealthy have tried to buy wisdom, but it was not for sale. Intellectuals have tried to understand it, but it only confused them. The famous have tried to laud it, but wisdom preferred to remain anonymous. Young people have declared that wisdom belonged to them, but wisdom has refused to be found in immediate pleasure, or by those who don't consider the consequences of their acts.

Some believed they could cultivate wisdom in laboratories, so they isolated themselves from the world and life's problems. But wisdom sought out common people and continued to grow amid real-world difficulties. Others have tried to cultivate wisdom with scientific and technological advances, but though science and technology have multiplied, the sorrows and flaws of the human soul have expanded.

Desperate, many people have tried to find ultimate answers by traveling to the farthest reaches of the universe. But they weren't in space; they didn't necessarily live in the highest buildings or inside palaces. Tired of searching, some scoffed: "A beautiful mind full of happiness, inspiration, creativity, security, and insight doesn't exist; it is a dream of those who never awaken."

The naysayers didn't prevent wisdom, however. It knocked at everyone's door. It was a sign of life for the oppressed and the cheerful, the depressed and the smiling, the ones who take action and the ones who live without masks. Whispering to the ears of the heart, it said softly: "Hey! I'm not in the world you're in, but in the world that you are!" Baffled, we cried out: "What? Speak louder!" Like the voice of a soft breeze it delicately whispered: "Don't try to find me in outer space or in the corners of the earth. Travel within yourself. I'm hidden in the roads of your emotions, in the core of your intellect . . . right now."

## The Purpose of Now

Now is the time to demand less of people and embrace our children, spouse, and friends more. It is time to tell them that they aren't the footnotes of our lives but the central pages of our stories. It is time to look into the eyes of those we love and apologize for our excessive work hours and our lack of sensitivity.

Now is the time to talk to our parents, discover their worlds, and open the chapters of their stories that we have never read before. It is time to ask them which were the most important nightmares and dreams in their lives.

Now is the time to face our weaknesses, reveal our "craziness," evaluate our priorities, and discover that life is wonderful but at the same time, very brief, and therefore we must live it intensely and with maturity. It is time to know that we are only human—imperfect people living among imperfect people—and that we do not have the capacity for being gods. It is time to cross over from our typical worlds to do something different, to relax and listen.

Now is the time to rescue lost dreams, rejuvenate our emotions, do the simple things that give us pleasure, and direct the scripts of our own stories. Now is the time to establish strategies to celebrate life.

## Dreams Become Reality

We need to change our stories, irrigate our emotions with generosity, and use our amazing minds and hearts to contribute to society. And we can!

While I was finalizing the preparations for this book for its publication in English, I received several messages. I chose two to represent people who are connecting with the Multi-Focal program and its Think Correctly principles. The first one that I found intriguing was sent by a human resources specialist. After reading this book, he has been inspired to greater heights of affection, compassion, creativity, and insight:

> Good afternoon, Dr. Cury. I'd like to share with you the gratitude and joy in my heart right now because of your teachings and wisdom. Ever since I read your book, my heart smiles and is overwhelmed and sings. . . .
>
> I've never seen anything like it . . . to renew my being. For a while now, my heart has been speaking to me about volunteer work with teenagers, and in this quest I found this book. . . . Your words speak directly to what my heart has been telling me about the true education of our being. While I read your pages, I felt an explosion of joy, ecstasy, and gratitude toward Existence for placing you at the head of such a special project. . . . I believe that it is a project for tomorrow and will spread throughout all cities and cultures.
>
> Life has shown me a new road. . . . It has placed me in this program, and I now begin my journey. . . . I will follow the signs and the direction that Existence shows me, making a path as I walk. Thank you for sharing your knowledge and touching our hearts so beautifully.

The second one says:

I have been a college professor in one of the most renowned universities in Brazil for over thirty years . . . but I confess that I was disillusioned with the university. In my opinion we had been forming repeaters of ideas and not thinkers with brilliant, creative, bold, secure, tranquil, imaginative, free, and enterprising minds. Our students were being prepared to face logical situations but were unprepared for the challenges of life. Their memories were cluttered with information but we weren't forming human beings capable of managing their thoughts, constructing new ideas, or acting as modifying agents of their life story and of society. Therefore, when I was able to incorporate Multi-Focal Psychology theory into my courses, I was excited. I saw a great opportunity to form thinkers.

I began by organizing several study groups with both graduate and postgraduate students. Every week we would discuss one of the program's principles. The results have been exciting. The students have begun to expand the horizon of their minds, protect their emotions, set their creativity free, and celebrate life and enrich its quality. Many of them have discovered that they have accelerated thought syndrome and have started to deal with it in a mature way. For the first time they have learned how to talk about themselves, how to use tools to become the protagonists of their own stories, and how to stop being the victims of their conflicts. Some of them had the courage to cry in front of their classmates, and others spoke of the difficulties that had been buried for years. They have learned that one can only be great in the social theater if one learns how to leave the audience, go onto the stage, and become healthy in the psychic theater. Thank you.[1]

I sincerely do not deserve this praise. Instead, I applaud all of those people who seek the richest life imaginable—for their own sake and the sake of others: people like these letter writers, who break from their indi-vidualism and become passionate about humanity in such a way that their minds reach the heights of thinking correctly.

## The Great Goal

As we've seen, the grand objective of the principles of this book is to change the direction in which societies are headed by changing the direc-tion in which people are headed. So we've questioned, reviewed, and examined everything we know and believe to arrive at twelve principles that can form a foundation for personal and societal change and allow us to progress in the brightest areas of our minds. And thousands and thou-sands of people and organizations are making it so.

Psychologists who are specialists in other theories are successfully using Multi-Focal Psychology and its principles in their practices. Teachers are using it in middle schools, high schools, and universities. Executives are using it in their companies. Spiritual leaders are using it among their people. I hope you will embrace the opportunity with all your heart.

Based on my experience, I believe the average mind has two or three of these twelve principles integrated into its personality and life to some degree. But for the rest of the principles, we are probably reading for the first time ideas that we should have been hearing since childhood. Fortu-nately, it is not too late—it is *never* too late to discover wisdom and the art of thinking. It is never too late to think correctly.

We have studied profound areas of the workings of the mind and the development of personality. We have learned how to enrich our minds, expand our wisdom, and transform our relationships into an oasis that will sustain life. We've traveled deeper into ourselves than we perhaps have ever traveled before with these twelve principles. Let me repeat them once more:

1. Be the author of your own story.
2. Direct your thoughts.

3. Manage your emotions.

4. Protect your memory.

5. Learn to listen and dialogue.

6. Learn to self-dialogue.

7. Contemplate beauty.

8. Unleash creativity.

9. Be restored in your sleep.

10. Live an enterprising lifestyle.

11. Think existentially.

12. Turn life into a celebration.

At the conclusion of each of the first eleven chapters, you worked through reflections and written assignments. But in this twelfth chapter there will be no concluding exercises. The heart of this chapter is a simple admonition: celebrate the adventure we call life! This chapter is your time to prepare to take what you have learned and apply it passionately to your life. Not to do so would be like going into a fine restaurant and eating the menu instead of the meal.

Your life is the biggest and most important institution in the world, and only you can keep it from spiritual and emotional bankruptcy. It is your responsibility to protect it from outside pressures and inner conflicts that might diminish its influence. Indeed, there are many people who admire you and depend on you. They need you to be healthy, free, happy, and wise.

If you are like most people, you are your own worst critic. You will likely never face the kinds of critics Jesus did, but you daily face one even more severe: yourself. But with what you have discovered in the Think Correctly principles, you can become your own best leader.

This program has shown you the direction, but only you can walk the path. It has given you the pen and paper, but only you can write your story. It has shown you how to use the wings of your incredible mind, but only you can soar.

## The Truth About Thinking Correctly

Remember, thinking correctly and the quality of life such thinking delivers is not having skies without storms, paths without accidents, work without fatigue, or relationships without disappointments. Instead, the Thinking Correctly life is knowing how to value smiles as well as sorrows. It is having humility in success and learning lessons from failures. It is being thankful for the applause while knowing that the best treasures are hidden within simple and anonymous things.

Thinking correctly is being aware that each human being is a world to be discovered and a story to be explored. Everyone has hidden riches within them, even the hardest and most complicated of people, even the ones who continuously err and fail. Dig for gold within the depths of those you love. Dig for gold within your own being. Few know how to find it; therefore, few live happy days.

Thinking correctly is not being afraid of your own feelings. It is having the maturity to say, "I was wrong," the courage to say, "Forgive me." It is being bold enough to be rejected by others without rejecting yourself; having the security to receive criticism even if it is unfair. Quality of life is making new friends but never leaving the old ones behind.

Thinking correctly is being a capable navigator in the waters of emotion, kissing your children constantly, embracing your parents affectionately, and looking into the eyes of one who is special to you and vibrantly saying, "I love you! I need you!" It is never giving up on people, even though they frustrate and disappoint us. And it is never forgetting that each person can achieve a brilliant, amazing, powerful, competent, remarkable, leading, humble, dream-filled, and free mind.

Each morning we can live the spectacle of life. Knowing how to use psychological tools to find emotional riches in loss, strength in forgiveness, security in despair, experience in fear, and joy in pain makes it possible.

Thinking correctly is not for heroes or giants, but for people who discover that above all else, having the highest quality of life is having the conviction that despite our failures, crises, flaws, difficulties, and tears, life is a unique drama in the theater of existence. Go after it with all that you are!

# The Brevity of Life Demands Wisdom

How did gold and precious stones become the most valuable commodities on earth? They are rare and hard to come by. In that, they perfectly illustrate this maxim: that which is in shortest supply is valued most.

If that is true, why don't we value our lives above all other things? Measured against the eons of earth's history, our seventy to one hundred years on this earth are but the blink of an eye. That brevity suggests we should value our lives far more than we do—that we should be gleaning from them every joy and pleasure that is possible to discover and experience. Yet because we lose sight of the big picture, we put off till "tomorrow" those choices and actions that will lead to health in the long run.

Being wise doesn't mean being perfect. The best definition of wisdom is from the ancient Hebrew culture, where wisdom meant skill. If one was a gifted artisan or craftsman, he was said to be "wise." Therefore, wisdom in life means living life skillfully. It means knowing how to respond to every event life brings—positive or negative, hurtful or helpful, joyful or sorrowful. It means knowing how to pilot your life as a ship captain pilots his craft, avoiding the shoals and hidden dangers that only the skilled eye can see.

# Who Will Benefit from This Book

"Thinking correctly" means becoming the author of one's own story, becoming capable of contemplating beauty, finding pleasure in living, enjoying refreshing sleep and rest, breaking free from the prison of destructive emotions, being enterprising and creative, and building and sustaining healthy relationships. Do you know anyone who would not profit from such a mind-set?

If you're still not sure, consider the following list of symptoms that are commonly found in modern societies, and note how many of them you experience. Then see where you stand at the end. (Note: this is the test I gave the doctors on the cruise ship—see chapter 2.)

## Psychological Symptoms

- Exaggerated fatigue
- Accelerated thoughts
- Insomnia
- Drowsiness
- Forgetfulness
- Lack of motivation
- Discouragement
- Diminishing sexual pleasure
- Low self-esteem
- Fear
- Loss of pleasure in living
- Sadness or depressive moods
- Lack of concentration
- Suffering by anticipation
- Anguish (anxiety + tight chest)
- Aggressiveness
- Intense feelings of guilt
- Loneliness
- Thoughts of giving up on life

## Psychosomatic Symptoms

- Headaches
- Breathlessness
- Dizziness
- Tachycardia (elevated heart rate)
- Knotted throat

- Chest tightness
- Muscular pain
- Prurigo (itchiness)
- Gastritis
- Hypertension when tense
- Diarrhea when tense
- Increased appetite (or diminished appetite)
- Excessive sweating
- Crying or the desire to cry
- Cold or sweaty hands
- Hair loss

The more symptoms a person is experiencing from either category, the more diminished is one's quality of life:

**0 symptoms:** Excellent quality of life
**1–2 symptoms:** Good quality of life
**3–4 symptoms:** Ordinary quality of life
**5–9 symptoms:** Poor quality of life
**10 or more symptoms:** Severely diminished quality of life

This classification is not rigid, of course. It merely illustrates why some people experience a lesser quality of life.

If you are experiencing none of the symptoms above, you should still absorb the material in this book in order to strengthen and sustain the quality of life you have and to be able to gain expertise with which you can help others. If your quality of life is anything less than excellent, you can make significant moves toward improving it by working through the twelve chapters of this book.

# For Small Group and Classroom Use

While the Think Correctly principles can be used on an individual basis, applying these principles in a group setting is one of the main goals of this book.

As the title suggests, *Think and Make It Happen* is intellectually interactive, allowing for the exchange of experiences between readers. When used in a small group, it produces mutual learning opportunities and the chance to build a fascinating network of social relationships. Such interaction and accountability encourages the practice of the Think Correctly principles and stimulates social and psychological health in a way that can't be duplicated in isolation. However, if you wish to work through it as an individualized program, go back to the beginning of the book and begin again, step by step, week after week. Then, in the twelfth week, gather those you love and prepare a pleasant dinner for them. If the program was good for you, encourage them to practice it. It will be an act of love toward them.

## Interested in Facilitating?

This book offers a precious opportunity for the psychological training, emotional education, and intellectual development of the most important functions of the mind. Many people have used the Multi-Focal program and these twelve principles to better their lives, including doctors, teachers, patients, students, parents, spiritual leaders, and employers. So no matter who you are, you can form small groups in your school, company, family, or church. And if you want to lead a group like this, and you have a heart for this discovery process, then pursue it.

Facilitating doesn't mean you have to be the most capable person in the group. It isn't necessary to have a college degree, be a health worker, or be an educator either, although these professionals are welcome. What is required is having life experience and the motivation to help others discover and develop their amazing minds.

If you've decided to accept the challenge, then congratulations on your love for life. You are sure to be rewarded in many ways for participating in this dream, for giving to others, and for doing your part so that humanity can be a little better.

## Before the First Meeting

- Seek to assemble a group of at least ten to fifteen people if possible.
- Ideally, you will have twelve meetings—one for each Think Correctly principle.
- Each group should have a facilitator who will be responsible for the practical aspects: publicizing the group, keeping meetings on schedule, establishing the time and location of the first meeting, etc. (The facilitator should encourage the development of new facilitators during the program. After the end of each course, the new leaders can form their own groups within their circles of contact.)
- During the meetings the facilitator's main role is not to control the group but to moderate the exchange of experiences and ideas. A mind that thinks correctly loves to promote the growth of others. The facilitator should read this book at least two or three times to be familiar with it, and before each meeting, should

review the "Suggested Topics" section at the end of each chapter. This can serve as a general topical outline and help the facilitator encourage the sharing of ideas and experiences within the group.

- It is recommended that each participant get his or her own copy of the book to study, take notes in, and complete the homework.
- Ask all participants to read the introduction and appendix A. (The first meeting will begin with exploring the first Think Correctly principle.)

## Meeting Guidelines for Facilitators

- Conduct a ninety-minute meeting for twelve weeks. The group will discuss one Think Correctly principle each week, except for Week 12. See the last item in this list for an explanation.
- It would be ideal if there were instrumental music being played in the background during the meetings, but it's not a rule. Music is relaxing and opens the windows of memory.
- Greet each group member before each meeting, and encourage the other members to do the same.
- Start on time, and if possible, have all meetings held at the same time and in the same location.
- Have participants sit in a circle or a U formation so that they can see each other's faces. Remember that facial expressions and body language say as much or more than words.
- *For the first meeting:* Give a brief synopsis of the Multi-Focal program and the twelve principles in this book, introduce the members of the group, discuss group expectations, explain the structure and schedule of meetings, etc. Remind everyone that confidentiality, respect, and understanding are crucial. In such an environment, talking about our hurtful experiences relieves us and gives us the tools to prevail. Also, mention that learning to listen is even more important than speaking. The members shouldn't require eloquence from each other; but if everyone is paying

attention, they can extract gold from the simplest of experiences.

- *Phase I of each meeting (15–20 minutes):* Summarize each chapter, enriching it with your own experiences and highlighting key thoughts from your reading. You may also want to read aloud excerpts from the chapter, or ask willing group members to read the excerpts.

- *Phase II of each meeting (60 minutes):* After your summary, open the discussion to the group. This is the most important phase. Encourage each member to

  1. give opinions;
  2. expose his or her experiences;
  3. talk about his or her difficulties for no more than five minutes. If someone exceeds the time limit, politely tell that person that he or she has another minute to conclude. In this way, even the most timid person can have a chance to participate. (Note: Don't forget the Think Correctly tenet that *those who are fragile hide their mistakes; the strong recognize them.* As the facilitator, be willing to be the first one to courageously share your feelings: "I need to improve in this area . . ." "I have this difficulty . . ." The participants who do not wish to speak don't have to, but the more people participate, the better their quality of life will be. Keep in mind, too, that if a member has had an experience that he or she considers compromising and prefers never to discuss it in the group, he or she should be encouraged to seek the help of a psychologist.) Affirm and thank each member after that individual shares, and make sure the group applauds when someone tells his or her experiences.

- *Phase III of each meeting (10–15 minutes):* Do a quick review of this week's principle. Give a short wrap-up that includes directing members to explore on their own the "Exercises and Reminders" section at the end of each chapter (which contains material that all participants should be encouraged to apply during the week). Then assign the next chapter for reading. Encourage participants not to just read but to study next week's principle ahead of time.

- Because an accomplished mind encourages others in the best way, have a round of applause at the end of each meeting. That way everyone can send each other off with wishes for an excellent week of practicing the latest Think Correctly principle.
- *(Week 12):* At the final group meeting, have a wonderful party with all the members participating. Notify the group about it ahead of time so that members can invite their friends, children, parents, neighbors, colleagues—in other words, anyone they hold dear. It should be a happy event that can also include games and decorations.

Read or talk about the text in chapter 12, with beautiful music playing in the background. This shouldn't take more than fifteen minutes. Next, ask the group members to come up to the front. With the music continuing to play quietly, encourage each participant to take two minutes to talk about or read an excerpt, outlining the most important things they learned or experienced while participating in this project. (Again, notify them of this in Week 11 so they can prepare.) They can also share what they expect about how their lives will be from now on.

After these testimonies, encourage the guests to form new groups, commenting that participation is free of charge and that the only cost is the book. The members of the group should pass around registration forms containing a few important phrases taken from this book and giving each guest a flower. (People are invited with flowers because life should be a garden.) After handing out all the invitations, the invitees should be applauded and greeted by the members of the graduating group as a welcoming gesture. Finally, read out loud this message from Dr. Cury:

Esteemed friends:

Congratulations on taking this long journey. These principles have laid a road that you can travel throughout your life, till your final breath. I only hope that the quality of life principles you have studied here can become your life-project.

The twelfth Think Correctly principle is to make life a great celebration and an eternal adventure. Today you aren't studying this principle; you are living it in a celebration of brotherhood and sisterhood, because life should be constantly celebrated.

This is a moment to enter the territory of emotion and understand the greatness and levity of life. I hope that through this experience, new groups will be formed and new facilitators found, and that the facilitator of this group will continue his or her journey with another group so that we can all learn to be passionate about life and have a love affair with it. The Multi-Focal program is indeed a love affair with life. May these twelve principles on thinking correctly lead you to live and love as never before, and give you the happiness you seek.

With kind regards,
Augusto Cury

After this, the food and fun can commence.

## Using the Multi-Focal Program as a Course Discipline in Schools

Besides encouraging the practice of this program in small groups, schools and universities (including postgraduate programs) are encouraged to adopt this book and include the Multi-Focal program as a course in their curriculum.

It is best for each school to have a teacher, regardless of his or her specialization, who has the characteristics of a small-group facilitator (see above) and who has studied this book. If possible, the teacher should divide each chapter into two classes:

1st class: Presentation of the Think Correctly principle;

2nd class: Presentation of the "Model of Thinking Correctly" ( Jesus of Nazareth) material.

It should be reiterated to students a number of times that the classes on Jesus' model of quality of life are a study of applied psychology and not religion. They include time-tested material for every human being of any persuasion—including students who consider themselves to be atheists—because of the references to the scientific study of Jesus' personality: how he lived each principle and how he developed the principles in his students, thereby creating thinkers.

After a thirty-minute presentation, the teacher should open the discussion to allow an exchange of experiences among the students. Consider using the first series of questions and comments at the end of each chapter as a guideline. The second list could be used as homework.

This new discipline does not exclude the possibility of students participating in other Multi-Focal groups in the format already covered, for the themes are complex and inextinguishable. In the face of the worldwide educational crisis, Multi-Focal Psychology can provide students a great opportunity to improve their minds and become excellent thinkers. Yet this book also includes all the great themes of life education: training in peace, stewardship, health, the exercise of human rights, and the practice of citizenship.

Whether the material in this book is taught in twenty-four classes or less, it is a short time for such great gains! Students gain access to knowledge that can help prevent depression, suicide, pharmacological dependencies, anxiety, stress, phobias, timidity, and violence. The systematic study and application of these principles also contributes to the formation of sympathetic, tolerant, sociable, affectionate, creative, wise, and enterprising leaders for tomorrow. Think of the leap in quality of life that our children and our society would have if this material finds an even greater place in academia.

In any case, it is my belief that this program realizes the dream of Moses, Mohammed, Confucius, Augustine, Plato, Piaget, Freud, Paulo

Freire, Einstein . . . in other words, all the great thinkers of history: the dream of forming free and mature human beings.

You may e-mail Dr. Cury at instituto.academia@uol.com.br.

# Notes

INTRODUCTION

1. See my book *Inteligência Multifocal* (Sao Paulo: Cultrix, 1998).

CHAPTER ONE

1. Isaiah 50:7.
2. See Matthew 27:18.
3. See Luke 6:8.
4. See John 2:24–25.
5. See John 8:1–11.
6. John 8:7.
7. Luke 9:54.

CHAPTER TWO

1. I have written a book that has been published in more than forty countries to alert societies to the epidemic of ATS: *Pais Brilhantes—Professores Fascinantes* (Rio de Janeiro: Sextante, 2004).
2. See my book *The Future of Humanity* (São Paulo: Sextante, 2005).
3. Matthew 6:34.

CHAPTER THREE

1. See John 7.
2. John 7:46.

3. See Matthew 27:54.

4. Matthew 26:38.

5. See Luke 22:44.

## Chapter Four

1. See John 13:26.

2. John 13:27.

3. See Matthew 26:31–34, 69–75.

4. Matthew 26:50; Luke 22:48.

5. See Matthew 5:39.

## Chapter Five

1. See Matthew 26:36–38.

2. John 10:10.

## Chapter Six

1. See Matthew 15:1–20.

2. Matthew 15:11 (my paraphrase).

3. Matthew 15:12.

4. Matthew 15:13–15.

5. Matthew 15:16 (my paraphrase).

## Chapter Seven

1. Contemporary literary references to the term *psychoadaptation* can be found, among other places, in the September 27, 1971, *Time* magazine article "Psychoadaptation, or How to Handle Dissenters," referencing Russian scientist and author Zhores Medvedev. It reported that a primary fear of Medvedev's was that the Soviet government at that time was possibly experimenting with "a sinister new form of repression"—which he termed "psychoadaptation"—"as a means of controlling dissent." Various researchers use the term very differently from its use and meaning in Multi-Focal Psychology theory and this book.

2. See Matthew 5–7.

3. Matthew 6:26, 28.

4. See Mark 7:14–15.

CHAPTER EIGHT

1. Luke 22:61.

2. E.g., Matthew 7:28; 8:27; 9:33; 13:54; 15:31; 21:20; 22:22.

3. E.g., Matthew 8:2–3; Mark 14:3; Luke 17:11–19.

4. See Luke 7:34.

5. See Luke 19:2–8.

CHAPTER NINE

1. Ephesians 4:26 (my paraphrase).

2. See Matthew 8:23–26.

3. See Matthew 8:20.

4. Luke 23:34 KJV.

CHAPTER TEN

1. See Luke 23:34.

CHAPTER ELEVEN

1. See Luke 14:7–11.

2. See John 6:53–71.

3. John 6:68.

CHAPTER TWELVE

1. Personal correspondence from Dr. Paulo Franceseline, professor, Universitad Estado de Sau Paulo. Used by permission.

# Bibliography

Adler, Alfred. *A Ciência da Natureza Humana (The Science of Human Nature)*. São Paulo: Editora Nacional, 1957. [New York: Fawcett, 1963]

Adorno, Theodor W. *Educação e emancipação (Education and Emancipation)*. Rio de Janeiro: Paz e Terra, 1971.

Amen, Daniel G. *Healing the Hardware of the Soul*. New York: Simon & Schuster, 2002.

Arendt, Hannah. *Entre o passado e o futuro (Between Past and Future)*. São Paulo: Perspectiva, 1972. [New York: Penguin, 1993]

———. *Condição humana (The Human Condition)*. Rio de Janeiro: Forense. 1993. [Chicago: University of Chicago, 1998]

Aristóteles (Aristotle). *Acerca del alma (About the Soul)*. Madrid: Edição trilíngue, 1974.

Baars, Bernard J., and Nicole M. Gage, *Cognition, Brain, and Consciousness*. San Diego: Academic Press/Elsevier, 2007.

Bastin, Ted, et al. *Quantum Theory and Beyond*. New York: Cambridge University Press, 1971.

Cury, Augusto J. *O Mestre dos Mestres (Master of Masters)*. São Paulo: Academia de Inteligência, 1999.

———. *O Mestre Inesquecível (Unforgettable Master)*. São Paulo: Academia de Inteligência, 2003.

———. *Inteligência Multifocal (Multi-focal Intelligence)*. São Paulo: Editora Cultrix, 1998.

———. *Treinando a Emoção para ser Feliz (Training Your Emotion to Be Happy)*. São Paulo: Academia de Inteligência, 2001.

———. *Pais Brilhantes–Professores Fascinantes (Brilliant Parents, Fascinating Teachers)*. São Paulo: Sextante, 2003.

Damásio, Antonio. *O Mistério da Consciência (The Mystery of Consciousness)*. São Paulo: Companhia das Letras, 2000.

Descartes, René. *Discurso do Método (Discourse on Method)*. Brasília: Editora da Universidade de Brasília, 1981. [Publisher: Digireads.com (January 1, 2005)]

Durant, Will. *História da Filosofia (The Story of Philosophy)*. Rio de Janeiro: Nova Fronteira, 1996. [Publisher: Pocket (January 1, 1991)]

Foucaut, Michael. *Microfísica do Poder (The Power of Microphysics)*. Rio de Janeiro: Graal, 1986.

Frankl, Victor. E. *A Questão do Sentido em Psicoterapia (The Question of Direction in Psychotherapy)*. Campinas, São Paulo: Papirus, 1990.

Freud, Sigmund. *Obras Psicológicas Completas de Sigmund Freud (Complete Psychological Works of Sigmund Freud)*. Rio de Janeiro: Imago, 1969. [Publisher: Vintage; New Ed edition (September 20, 2001)]

Fromm, Erich. *Análise do Homem (On Being Human)*. Rio de Janeiro: Zahar, 1960. [Publisher: Continuum International Publishing Group (March 1, 1997)]

Gardner, Howard. *Inteligências Múltiplas (Multiple Intelligences)*. Porto Alegre: Artes Médicas, 1995. [Publisher: Basic Books (July 3, 2006)]

Goleman, Daniel. *Inteligência Emocional (Emotional Intelligence)*. Rio de Janeiro: Objetiva, 1996. [Publisher: Bantam; 10 Anv edition (September 26, 2006)]

Husserl, Edmund. *A Idéia da Fenomenologia (The Idea of Phenomenology)*. Lisboa: Edições 70, 1986. [Publisher: Springer; 1 edition (April 30, 1999)]

Jung, Carl G. *Obras Completas (Complete Works)*. Petrópolis: Editora Vozes, 1997. [Publisher: Pantheon (1956)]

———. *O Desenvolvimento da Personalidade (The Development of the Personality)*. Petrópolis: Vozes, 1961. [*The Integration of the Personality* may be the English translation of this book. Publisher: Routledge & Kegan Paul (1956)]

Kaplan, Harold I., Benjamin, J. Sadock, and Jack A. Grebb. *Compêndio de Psiquiatria: Ciência do Comportamento e Psiquiatria Clínica (Compendium of Psychiatry: Psychiatry and Behavioral Science Clinic)*. Porto Alegre: Artes Médicas, 1997. [*Synopsis of Psychiatry : Behavioral Sciences Clinical Psychiatry* is the English translation. Publisher: Williams & Wilkins; 7 Sub edition (April 1994) ]

Kierkegaard, Soren. *Os Pensadores—Kierkegaard (The Thinkers)*. São Paulo: Abril, 1951. [Publisher: Harper (1959)]

Lipton, Bruce. *The Biology of Belief.* Santa Rosa, California: Mountain of Love/Elite Books, 2005.

Locker, Kitty O. *Business and Administrative Communication.* New York: McGraw-Hill, 2006.

Machado, Roberto. *Nietzsche e a Verdade (Nietzsche and Truth)*. Rio de Janeiro: Rocco, 1985.

McInerny, D. Q. *Epistemology.* Elmhurst, PA: The Priest Fraternity of St. Peter, 2007.

Morin, Edgar. *Os sete saberes necessários à educação do futuro (The Seven Knowledges Needed for the Education of the Future) (Relatório feito a pedido da UNESCO—Report Done the Order of UNESCO)*. São Paulo: Cortez/ Unesco, 2000.

Plato. *"República, Livro VII" (The Republic: Book VII)*. Paris: Lês Belles Lettres, 1985.

Rogers, Carl. *Sobre o Poder Pessoal (On Personal Power)*. São Paulo: Martins Fontes, 1986. [Publisher: Delta Books (1978)]

Skinner, B. F. *O comportamento verbal (Verbal Behavior)*. São Paulo: Cultrix Edusp, 1978. [Publisher: Copley Publishing Group (December 1, 1991)]

Vigotsky, L. *A formação social da mente (The Social Formation of the Mind)*. São Paulo: Martins Fontes, 1987.

# Index